PRAISE FOR
THE ENTREPRENEUR'S EDGE

"Scott Becker is one of the smartest and most focused business people out there. The ability to spot complexity and ask smart questions to get to simplicity while connecting dots quickly is uncanny. Any businessperson or leader should read this practical and jam packed book full of amazing concepts and ideas."

JESSICA COLE
Chief Executive Officer and President, Becker's Healthcare

"From building enduring businesses, to recruiting talent to building new categories, I along with many other entrepreneurs have been fortunate enough to hear these lessons directly from Scott Becker over the past decade. Scott's inspiration, wisdom and earned secrets have not only helped me and others accelerate our professional dreams, but have also helped us personally become better people in the process. I couldn't be more excited for the "John Wooden" of healthcare to finally share his wisdom with the world."

VENKAT MOCHERLA
Co-Founder, Midstream Health

"I have known Scott Becker for more than 30 years. Scott has a wealth of knowledge and common sense. He has guided and advised me throughout most of my career. Scott is a selfless servant leader, an incredible human being, and someone whom I am proud to call my friend."

BARRY TANNER
Chief Executive Officer, Integrated Oncology Network
Former Chief Executive Officer, PE GI Solutions (Physicians Endoscopy)
Board Member of Several PE GI Sponsored Companies

"Scott has helped me understand the value of investing in relationships. Investing time in building meaningful relationships with people that have similar values has been critical to our growth and Scott's guidance in how to do this has been invaluable. He has and continues to be a trusted advisor personally and professionally."

MANAV SEVAK
Founder and CEO, Memora Health

"I look forward to reading Scott's email newsletter and listening to his podcasts. The newsletter provides a brief update on topics of the day. The podcasts cover a range of topics that help me improve my leadership skills, educate on topics in the business field or just provide perspective on a everyday/non-business topics. I consider both great and necessary investments of time."

ANDY PAULSON
Executive Director, Central Illinois Endoscopy Center

"Scott was the keynote at the SMISS Annual Meeting. As usual, he gave a phenomenal talk on the state of healthcare in the US with a bend towards spine care. His lecture was insightful and extremely thought provoking. There is nobody I know who delivers more interesting and educational lectures in this arena."

DR. FRANK PHILIPS, M.D.
Founder, Board Member, the Society of Minimally Invasive Spine Surgery

Professor of Orthopedic Surgery, University of Chicago
Orthopaedic Surgeon, Midwest Orthopaedics at Rush University Medical Center

"As an entrepreneur, Scott Becker was and is a mentor for my healthcare business. Following his publications, podcasts, conferences and books has been instrumental in the success of nimble solutions in the beginning and through explosive growth and to me personally and professionally. If you work in healthcare in any capacity - you need him."

LISA ROCK
Founder and Long Time President, National Medical Billing Services (NMBS)
Executive Advisor, Nimble Solutions

"Scott Becker has an impactful way of diving into relevant topics with his audience. He is truly the best interviewer I have ever come across - his ability to make strategic connections and emerge with profound business and life insights is unparalleled. His podcasts are succinct and pack a powerful punch. Such a great way to quickly get educated on current themes and events in our world."

ELIZABETH GEORGE HUTSON
Owner, Principal Consultant EGH, LLC

"Scott joined us as a Keynote for the BOMA medical conference to talk with us about the trends in Healthcare and Healthcare real estate. I had previously heard him speak at our DOC Summit and we enjoyed him a lot. He was able to take a subject that can be dry and made it fun and engaging. Scott is always full of joy and humor in presenting any subject matter. We truly appreciated his involvement and had great feedback from everyone at the conference."

AMY HALL
Senior Vice President, Healthpeak

"Scott is an inspirational leader and entrepreneur. He is able to see the big picture with clarity while never losing track of the critical blocking and tackling tasks. The most important lesson I learned from Scott is to focus on protecting talent and give top performers space and resources to thrive. This book is a great distillation of the lessons I have received over the last 15 years!"

HOLLY BUCKLEY
Chair of Health Care, McGuireWoods LLP

The

ENTREPRENEUR'S
EDGE

TK Atelier Business Publishing
Sbecker@beckerstrategygroup.com

ISBN: 979-8-9905661-0-1 (paperback)
ISBN: 979-8-9905661-1-8 (ebook)

Library of Congress Control Number: 2024912434

Ordering Information:
Special discounts are available on quantity purchases by corporations, associations,
and others. For details, contact Sbecker@beckerstrategygroup.com.

The ENTREPRENEUR'S EDGE

HOW TO BUILD, GROW, AND MANAGE YOUR BUSINESS

SCOTT BECKER *with* GRACE LYNN KELLER

TABLE OF CONTENTS

SECTION 1

So, You Want to Be an Entrepreneur?
Building a Great Business. 3

1. Most Entrepreneurs Should Work a Regular Job First   5
2. Two Secrets to Business Success   7
3. 15 Key Concepts in Building a Business   11
4. More on the Three Fundamental Orientations
   (the "Centrics")   15
5. Your Core Customer   17
6. It's Not About What You Want, It's About What the
   Customer Needs   19
7. Is It True That the Riches Are in the Niches?   21
8. Are You Building a Software as a Service Company?   23

SECTION 2

Now What (or Rather, WHO)?
Building Great Teams 25

9. The Simple Trick to Great Management—Hire and
   Retain Great People   27
10. Build Great Teams, Cultivate Multiple Leaders   31
11. Sorting Out People and Teams   33
12. 11 Essentials for Attracting, Engaging, and Retaining
    the Best People   35
13. Your Best People Will Have Ups and Downs   39
14. Recruit, Retain, and Automate   41
15. 11 Thoughts on Hiring, Promotion, and Retention   43

SECTION 3

Do You Have What It Takes?
Becoming a Great Leader 47

16. The Founder's Evolution in Three Stages   49
17. Analyzing vs. Acting in Management and Business   51
18. Grateful and High Praise, No Blame Cultures   53
19. Failure Is Fine … Within Reason   57
20. Three Keys to Judging Leaders   59

SECTION 4

Can You Get from Here to There?
Scaling a Business 61

21. You Need to Understand Your Own Business!   65
22. How to Grow a Company—Organic Growth vs.
    Mergers and Acquisitions   67
23. Pivots Are the Norm   69
24. Take Shots at the Plate   73
25. Focus on Core Competencies; Outsource
    Everything Else   75
26. Simplicity Is the Name of the Game   79
27. Don't Become Too Reliant on One Person or Customer   81
28. The Importance of Setting Key Priorities   83
29. Set Goals That Are Realistic and Winnable,
    Not Ego-Driven   85

SECTION 5

Is This It??
Finding Enduring Success 87

30. An Important Note on Physical and Mental Health   89
31. The Power of Saying No   91
32. Learn to Tune Out the Naysayers   93
33. Passion Is the Secret Ingredient   95

34. "I Have To" vs. "I Get To"   97
35. Digging Ditches   99
36. Obsess to Win and Excel   101
37. How to Turn Around from Failure When You're Young   103
38. Set Your Direction for Success and Satisfaction in a
Professional Services Firm   105

SECTION 6

So, You Want to Live the Dream?
Starting Out as a Young Professional 107

39. Building Something Great Requires Serious
Commitment and Effort   109
40. Three Tips for Emerging Professionals   111
41. Career Advice for Your First Job   113
42. Coachability, Commitment, and Career Success   115

SECTION 7

But How Do You Build Real Wealth?
Becoming a Great Investor 117

43. Five Pieces of Advice for the New Investor   119
44. Nine Overriding Rules on Investing   121
45. Allocation and Understanding Your Own Mindset Is
Everything   123
46. "Core and Explore" Investment Strategy   127
47. Know Your Investments   129
48. Time in the Market vs. Timing the Market   131
49. Three Types of Portfolios   133
50. Do Not Borrow to Invest in Stocks   135
51. What About Bond Yields?   137
52. The Two Types of Risk in Bonds—Duration or
Interest Rate Risk and Credit Risk   139
53. 10 Notes on Private Equity vs. Venture Capital   141

SECTION 8

Freedom for Life?

Becoming Financially Wise 145

54. Live Within Your Means; Pay Yourself First   147
55. Have a Job or Business and Put Money Away Outside
    the Job or Business   149
56. If You Want to Be Rich   151
57. Emergency Funds Are Critical   153
58. Six Ways to Prepare for a Recession   155
59. Six Key Concepts for Retirement   157
60. The 4% Rule   159

Acknowledgments   161
About the Authors   163

INTRODUCTION

THANK YOU FOR picking this book up. Thank you very much.

We talk in this book about two different but related subjects. First, we discuss key concepts in building businesses. Second, we talk about managing your money. Here, this discussion about money is more on the personal side than on the business side.

When it comes to building businesses, my core professional and business life revolved around building a healthcare media company and a healthcare business legal practice. Both were done with great partners and teams, and both required focusing on niche areas, developing great leaders and teams, and taking great care of clients, customers, and audiences. Each required a good deal of drive and motivation. Both were hard and both were labors of love. We constantly use the phrases niche-centric, team-centric, and customer-centric to describe how we view the core of building businesses.

As to managing money, I have had the chance to visit with many people in financial trouble and many who have done very well. This has led to the development of a whole number of core principles around money management. I am not a money manager, and most in that business would say I'm way too conservative. However, one very key part of investing is to understand, as well as you can, your own ability to deal with ups and downs, gains and losses. I don't deal with the downs that well and am more focused on safety. As someone who made money as an entrepreneur, I'm very cognizant of how hard or even impossible it would be to do again if I lost that money through high-risk investing.

I have been really fortunate along the way to work with great customers, leaders, colleagues, mentors, and investors. I'm crazily thankful. Thank you for reading.

P.S. Through these efforts, I have also had the chance to interview President George and Laura Bush and President Bill and Hillary Clinton as well as Nikki Haley, Kareem Abdul-Jabbar, and many others. We also had the chance to serve as a moot court advisor to President Barack Obama when we were both in law school. The president, even though I was the advisor/teacher, was far more gifted than me.

······· *Section 1* ·······

SO, YOU WANT TO BE AN ENTREPRENEUR?

············

BUILDING A GREAT BUSINESS

···································

SO, YOU WANT TO BE AN ENTREPRENEUR? (CHAPTERS 1–8)

Many people want to be entrepreneurs and start their own businesses. For many, being an entrepreneur and running your own business is part of the American Dream. Entrepreneurs are often celebrated and receive adulation, and when people think about entrepreneurs, they picture entrepreneurial successes like Steve Jobs, Elon Musk, or Oprah Winfrey.

However, being an entrepreneur is not easy.

Data from the Bureau of Labor Statistics (BLS) shows that approximately 20% of new businesses fail during their first 2 years, 45% during the first 5 years, and 65% during the first 10 years. Only 25% of new businesses survive 15 years or more.[1]

For those who want to be an entrepreneur, the bottom line is it is extremely hard and most new businesses fail. The following chapters provide some lessons from our experience that we believe can improve your chances of success.

---

1   Michael T. Deane, "Top 6 Reasons New Businesses Fail," Investopedia, December 30, 2022, https://www.investopedia.com/financial-edge/1010/top-6-reasons-new-businesses-fail.aspx#:~:text=Data%20from%20the%20BLS%20shows,to%2015%20years%20or%20more.

········· **1** ·········

MOST ENTREPRENEURS SHOULD WORK A REGULAR JOB FIRST

PEOPLE HAVE LEARNED to romanticize entrepreneurs like Steve Jobs, Mark Zuckerberg, Bill Gates, and Debbi Fields (founder of Mrs. Fields Cookies). Those who did not finish college and built a great business without ever working a "regular" job.

But most people gain a ton of knowledge and experience from their first job. They learn good habits, how to get things done, how to work with people, and much more. Students may romanticize the entrepreneur who left school early to start a company, but entrepreneurs who should leave school early are extremely rare. The odds of great success are very low. We view it as akin to a great athlete who does not go to college or the minor leagues before going pro. It may work, but rarely. Except for the once-in-a-generation geniuses like Steve Jobs or Bill Gates, most students with entrepreneurial aspirations should gain job experience before starting their company.

In reality, most successful entrepreneurs have started off with real jobs and have become what are commonly called "intrapreneurs" before becoming true entrepreneurs. They became business developers within their firms or businesses, and this role helped them hone their skills before leaving to start their own businesses.

Working a "regular job" can lead entrepreneurs to their first great business idea. It would be difficult to abstractly come up with an idea for a business without experience working in an industry and observing the challenges and opportunities that exist. By engaging in work for someone else, the aspiring entrepreneur gets hands-on experience with the needs of a particular niche, which may lead them to a business idea that solves the problems of this niche.

Famous entrepreneur Mark Cuban has said that young, aspiring entrepreneurs don't have to figure everything out at the beginning and their first jobs don't have to be their dream careers. Cuban recently said that no matter what your job is, "You're going to learn something new, you're going to network, and you're going to meet new friends."[2] Through these experiences, aspiring entrepreneurs acquire skills, learn what they love, and identify promising opportunities.

Many successful entrepreneurs have an innate talent for business, but it takes real-world work experience for these entrepreneurs to reach their full potential and gain the knowledge they need to eventually launch their first business.

---

2   Dustin McKissen, "Mark Cuban's 4-word advice to college grads might be the most comforting thing you hear today," CNBC, May 21, 2020. https://www.cnbc.com/2020/05/21/billionaire-mark-cuban-advice-to-college-grads-most-comforting-thing-you-hear-today.html.

·········· **2** ··········

TWO SECRETS TO BUSINESS SUCCESS

IN OUR EXPERIENCE, business success depends on two things:

1. *Formula/Vision/Goals.* A business needs a clear formula or mission for how goals will be executed. This formula may change some over time, but there does need to be some real clarity about what you're trying to achieve and how you're going to achieve it.

2. *People.* A business needs a constant focus on developing, hiring, promoting, and working with great people. Over time, your business will not work, improve, or sustain growth unless you hire, retain, and grow great people.

In whatever business you are in, you want to be able to clearly define the niche where you intend to fully excel.

In building a healthcare media business, our clear goal was to be the go-to information source for leaders of hospitals and health systems. We wanted to be a magnet for our readers, conference attendees, and podcast listeners. The formula that we created to achieve this goal was to develop high-quality, insightful, timely content about the business of healthcare that would be relevant and important to senior business leaders in hospitals, health systems, and other parts of healthcare.

In building a healthcare business and private equity legal practice, our goal was to be at the total center of that world and to be at the intersection of healthcare and private equity work. The formula that we used to achieve this goal was to hire top notch legal talent and provide outstanding services to healthcare organizations and private equity investors. The leaders who really drove the growth of the healthcare business and private equity legal practice include Geoff Cockrell, Thomas Zahn, Amber Walsh, Holly Buckley, Bart Walker, and more.

To accomplish both business goals, we needed great team members and great clarity about how we were to take care of clients and grow both our audience and reputation as leaders within these areas. We were also very focused on building very talented teams to pursue these goals as opposed to very large teams.

One of the greatest keys to success is to hire and build teams with people that can thrive and where many of them can far excel you, becoming leaders in their own right and often better leaders than you are yourself. We often try to judge a leader's success based on how many leaders and partners were created under their core leadership. The leader's own numbers and successes are important, but far more important is the number of new leaders that a person nurtures and mentors.

We also judge a leader based on how the organization does after the leader retires. For example, the success of Apple and Microsoft, post-Steve Jobs and Bill Gates, may be the greatest sign of their leadership success.

One more concept we think about constantly is how thriving for one's team and the company can be represented by a Venn diagram. In the Venn diagram, one circle is how the team members thrive personally and professionally and the second circle is how their actions help the company thrive. These circles overlap, but they need not overlap completely.

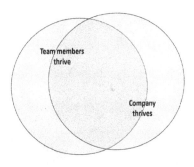

15 KEY CONCEPTS IN BUILDING A BUSINESS

IN THIS CHAPTER, we introduce the 15 key concepts in building a business. While all are important, the first three concepts listed below should be front and center in your mind as you build your business. These three concepts that rise above the others are being niche-centric, customer-centric, and people-and-team-centric.

1. *Niche-centric.* Define your niche as clearly as possible. It's much easier to focus on a narrow niche than a broad market. For example, a niche may be "We are the go-to place for information for health system leaders" or "We are the go-to place for clients completing healthcare transactions."

2. *Customer-centric.* Make sure you do everything you can to take care of your best customers. You want your best customers to feel valued. We strive to treat each one like our business is fully dependent on them.

* *

"If you work just for money, you'll never make it, but if you love what you're doing and you always put the customer first, success will be yours."
— *Ray Kroc, Founder, McDonald's*[3]

* *

3. *People-and-team-centric.* Similar to taking care of your customers, you need to build teams and take great care of your best people. We spend a huge amount of time and effort focused on cultivating leadership teams.

4. *Product-market fit.* You need a product or service that meets a customer's need, not just your needs.

5. *Scalability.* If you want to build a larger business, there must be some spots where 1 + 1 = 3. Linear scalability is difficult but doable. Can the business rely on systems and people and not be solely dependent on one great leader? Can it expand?

6. *Clarity of goals.* It's important to be able to clearly define what your business is great at (i.e., What does your business do better than everyone else?). It's critical to have clarity about what you want to achieve.

7. *Obsession with greatness.* At some point, the company will need to be intent and highly focused on its efforts. It's hard to be great without some level of obsession.

---

3   HelpScout, "101 Inspirational Customer Service Quotes," February 24, 2021. https://www.helpscout.com/customer-service-quotes/inspirational/.

8. *The evolution of the leader and founder.* The founder must be able to get the business going and find and build teams and leaders that are better at everything than him or her. He or she must commit to being less central to everything if the business is to grow and become great.

9. *Gratitude.* The best leaders are constantly thankful for their teams, people, and customers too. Communicating this is critical. It must be genuine.

10. *Know your own business.* The best leaders really know the ins and outs of their own company and their own area.

11. *Have a clear plan and be open to pivots.* This can be a great challenge for leaders and businesses. You must have clarity of goals and an open mind to changes. You can't make changes all the time. You must be very close to the business so you can see the pivots.

• •

*Harvard Business School Professor William Sahlman, who teaches entrepreneurship, has read over 10,000 business plans, but he's only seen three companies meet their plan. Success isn't about creating a business plan, it's about being able to **pivot** as you execute on the plan.*[4]

• •

---

[4]   Professor William Sahlman, "Everything I've learned in 37 years of studying Entrepreneurship," Global Silicon Valley YouTube Channel, March 2, 2019. https://www.youtube.com/watch?v=zh9fm4SrXk4.

12. *Apply 80-20 rules to people and customers.* Generally, you want to spend a huge percentage of your time on the people and customers that are most key to the business. This aligns with knowing your business and knowing very well who your best customers and people are.

13. *Apply 80-20 rules to the core business and new ideas.* It's critical to focus largely on what works and to have an open mind to new ideas. One needs to avoid chasing every single new idea. At some points, a business needs to heavily focus on execution as opposed to new ideas.

14. *Great systems and great ideas.* Great businesses have both great clarity as to how they do things and great people who can execute and improve the business.

15. *Great businesses know their core competencies.* They focus almost entirely on those and outsource everything else. Bain's textbook definition of a core competency is provided below. We think of a core competency as "What are we really great at."

Core Competencies Defined

According to Bain & Company, a core competency is a *deep proficiency that helps an organization deliver unique value to customers.* Core competencies are difficult for competitors to imitate, so they are often a source of competitive advantage.[5]

---

5 "Management Tools: Core Competencies," Bain & Company, April 2, 2018. https://www.bain.com/insights/management-tools-core-competencies/.

·········· **4** ··········

MORE ON THE THREE FUNDAMENTAL ORIENTATIONS (THE "CENTRICS")

WE CONSTANTLY THINK in terms of three core business concepts. We will talk a lot about these concepts throughout this book. The three concepts are:

1. Niche-centric
2. Customer-centric
3. People-and-team-centric

A niche can be defined in terms of:

- *Who* your business serves. For example, Becker's Healthcare serves leaders within health systems.

- *What* your business does. Becker's Healthcare serves its niche audience by providing cutting-edge business information and organizing industry events that promote knowledge-sharing and networking.

It is the combination of a narrow focus on exactly who you serve and extreme focus on exactly what you do that makes an organization niche-centric.

Niche-centric organizations find that it is a great deal easier to build a business around a small specific market segment than around a large broad market. For us, this has meant building a media company around specific, well-defined industry segments in healthcare rather than around a general consumer population.

Customer-centric means a heavy focus on taking care of a specific customer's needs. It also means focusing very heavily on satisfying your most important customers.

People-and-team-centric means you do everything you can to ensure your key people are thriving.

If you want to build a business, you need to be motivated to do so, you need to build great teams, and you need to build something that customers actually want or need. Mohan Giridharadas, the CEO of LeanTaaS, does a brilliant job of describing the need to build something customers need. Gary Guthart, the CEO of Intuitive—the developer of the DaVinci Robot—has done an amazing job of building great teams and building something that health systems need.

.... **5** ....

YOUR CORE CUSTOMER

WE SPEND A great deal of time, whether in a business-to-business firm or a consumer firm, trying to understand and take great care of a "core customer." Every successful business must readily understand the client and client group that drives the greatest percentage of profits and revenues. Here, it's a constant discipline to focus efforts around the 20% or so of customers that drive 80% of profits. The least important item for the most important customer is critically important.

In building a media business, we constantly track our top customers and constantly want to ensure they are thriving with us and we are meeting their expectations. This means constant huddles and constant tracking.

In building a legal practice, we have several core client meetings a week to make sure the core and important clients are taken care of very well.

In short, a business needs a constant focus on its most important customers, including team meetings and huddles to make sure key people are focused on key clients.

Creating a Core Customer Statement

In *The Inside Advantage: The Strategy That Unlocks the Hidden Growth in Your Business*, authors Robert Bloom and Dave Conti recommend creating a core customer statement that does the following:

- Captures the essence of your customer.
- Conveys that information in a brief, simple, clear statement.
- Goes beyond demographic terms when describing your customer—what are their needs, desires, and preferences?
- Expresses what your customer is looking for in the context of your products and services.
- Utilizes no more than 10 to 15 highly descriptive words to illustrate your core customer.[6]

---

6   Nedim Nisic, "Defining Your Core Customer: The Key to a Successful Digital Presence," LinkedIn, January 13, 2017. https://www.linkedin.com/pulse/defining-your-core-customer-key-successful-digital-presence-nisic/.

.... **6** ....

IT'S NOT ABOUT WHAT YOU WANT, IT'S ABOUT WHAT THE CUSTOMER NEEDS

THE MOST SUCCESSFUL businesses serve a real customer need. They are often built at the intersection of what a business is great at and what another business or customer needs. In contrast, many businesses are founded and pursued around a concept that is exciting to the founder. This is only one part of the game. To succeed, you need something that both the founder wants to do or produce *and* that the customer truly wants or needs.

We see many businesses start based on an idea the business or founder has. One of the mistakes we see founders make is not constantly and early on trying to commercialize that idea with customers. In other words, very early on, companies must test their ideas with customers and try to make sure whatever they are building or selling is truly needed and wanted by customers. Many companies spin their wheels because of the mismatch between what they are doing and what customers want.

. . . .

"We're not competitor obsessed, we're customer obsessed. We start with what the customer needs and we work backward."
    – Jeff Bezos, Chairman and CEO, Amazon.com[7]

. . . .

---

7   Ruth Umoh, "Jeff Bezos: When you find a business opportunity with these traits, 'don't just swipe right, get married,'" CNBC, September 14, 2018. https://www.cnbc.com/2018/09/13/amazon-jeff-bezos-4-traits-a-good-business-opportunity-should-have.html.

IS IT TRUE THAT THE RICHES ARE IN THE NICHES?

JACK WELCH, THE long-term CEO of GE, famously pushed the concept that if you are going to be in business, you should be first or second in that business or not be in that business. His concept is that the vast majority of the profits in all times go to the top one to two companies in an area and that in bad times, the top one to two tend to survive even if not making great profits.

Two key questions we often use to assess niches are:

1. *Can you win in the niche?* Key considerations include whether you can become a top player, whether the niche is clearly defined, and whether you have the resources to excel.

2. *Is the niche worth winning in?* Key considerations here are whether there are enough profits and revenues in the niche so you can succeed in a substantial way.

We believe it is much easier to develop a business around a niche. The total addressable market—the "TAM"—may be bigger in a general area compared to niche areas, but the chances of success are usually much better in a niche. Thus, it takes time and effort to truly define the niche, but this effort is important.

I remember having a mini heart attack—I embellish here, of course—whenever a new competitor entered into one of our markets. Over time, I used this as motivation to keep striving to win markets and be a leader in the businesses we were in. I still worry every day about new competitors, but my mini heart attacks have largely moved away.

. . . .

"Find a niche, not a nation."
— Seth Godin, The Bootstrapper's Bible[8]

. . . .

8   Seth Godin, "The Bootstrapper's Bible," Seth's Blog. https://seths.blog/wp-content/uploads/2013/09/8.01.bootstrappersbible-1.pdf.

········· **8** ·········

ARE YOU BUILDING A SOFTWARE AS A SERVICE COMPANY?

WHEN BUILDING A SaaS company, we ask leaders to focus fully on these three core things:

1. *Relentless focus on building great software.* It requires constant focus and consistent improvement. The software must truly meet a need and be highly adaptable. The first version has to be good, of course, but then you must dedicate your company to constant improvement, debugging, and updates over time.

2. *Relentless focus on commercialization.* Don't fall in love with the concept of building impressive software so much that it blinds you to the importance of commercialization. Early on, you must relentlessly commercialize so that you can actually sell and develop customers. The more often you beta test and put your software in front of customers, the better for your service's development

and sellability and your understanding of what customers really need.

3. *Understand which kind of software business you are in.* Are you selling an enterprise product that will be sold to only a few big customers? Are you selling a custom-developed product? Are you selling a mass-produced product? Understand which channel you are in, and in turn, which salespeople you need to be successful.

· ·

"To keep one's SaaS business safe from the 'chopping block,' understanding one's Customer Happiness Index and building a strategy to enhance it is essential. Organizations need to maintain a certain level of agility to ensure customer happiness and make it a point to listen to the customer every step of the way."
– Vineet Jain, Founder and CEO, Egnyte[9]

· ·

9   Vineet Jain, "Customer Happiness in the SaaS Business," LinkedIn, February 23, 2023. https://www.linkedin.com/pulse/customer-happiness-saas-business-vineet-jain%3FtrackingId=w%252FIRAauORoK6cpepjssnWg%253D%253D/?trackingId=w%2FIRAauORoK6cpepjssnWg%3D%3D.

····· *Section 2* ·······

NOW WHAT (OR RATHER, WHO)?

· · · · · · · · · · ·

BUILDING GREAT TEAMS

· ·

NOW WHAT (OR RATHER WHO)?
(CHAPTERS 9–15)

For almost any endeavor, success requires a team of capable, cooperative, motivated individuals. As Steve Jobs noted during a *60 Minutes* interview, "Great things in business are never done by one person. They're done by a team of people."[10]

The key to success is attracting and hiring great team members, engaging them in meaningful work, and helping them grow professionally. We like Reid Hoffman's (founder of LinkedIn) philosophy—"No matter how brilliant your mind or strategy, if you're playing a solo game, you'll always lose out to a team."[11]

We often talk about taking care of great people and great customers and also working to become less reliant on those great leaders and customers. At the same time, in any endeavor, you have to recognize your "ride or die" people that you never want to part with. If you're Apple, your "ride or die" is Steve Jobs—don't fire him or try to make him irrelevant. The same goes for Bill Belichick's decision that he should move forward without Tom Brady or Jerry Krause's decision to make a go without Michael Jordan. In any business, you have to recognize the "ride or die" people and do everything you can to support them and make sure they keep thriving with you. Jessica Cole gets a shoutout as a "ride or die" leader at Becker's Healthcare.

---

10 "Steve Jobs in his own words," CNET (republished on CBS News), October 6, 2011. https://www.cbsnews.com/news/steve-jobs-in-his-own-words/.

11 Megan Conley, "45 Quotes That Celebrate Teamwork, Hard Work, and Collaboration," HubSpot. https://blog.hubspot.com/marketing/teamwork-quotes.

THE SIMPLE TRICK TO GREAT MANAGEMENT—HIRE AND RETAIN GREAT PEOPLE

IT'S SIMILAR TO the trick of being a great coach. A great coach seems great if he or she recruits great players. This is not intended to understate what a manager does with that talent, but it's a lot easier to be a great manager with great people. It's often more about the people than the leader. Hire great people and use a light touch. If one doesn't prioritize the recruitment and retention of great people, then one needs to engage in a lot more micro-management. This is generally very limiting to a company's growth.

. . . .

"People are not your most important asset. The right people are."

— *Jim Collins, Good to Great*[12]

. . . .

In our experience, it's much easier to build great businesses with great people. When you identify great candidates or great employees, leaders must do everything they can to help those people thrive. A clear role of the leader is to cultivate and identify great performers. Most great firms start with a few great leaders and performers. A great business must retain and develop those people.

When we first started sorting out teams and people at Becker's Healthcare, one of our key actions was putting Jessica Cole in charge of growing and leading the team. At the time, Jessica was just a few years out of college, but she was outperforming everyone else. Fast forward to today and she is both CEO and President of Becker's Healthcare and was named the EY Transformational Executive of the Year in 2019. Don't shy away from sorting out teams and betting on great people.

An important part of betting on great people is recognizing uncommon integrity. Periodically we have a colleague—and I'll call out Bart Walker here—who shows uncommon integrity. Bart is now a leader at McGuireWoods. When he was a very young lawyer working on my team, he came to me and said, "Look, I know

---

12 Stefaan Stroo, "People are not your most valuable assets, the right people are," LinkedIn, December 12, 2019. https://www.linkedin.com/pulse/people-your-most-valuable-assets-right-stefaan-stroo/.

you are investing a lot of time in me and my development. I want you to know that sooner or later I'm moving back to Charlotte." He took a risk that I'd not keep him, if I knew that he would be relocating. His uncommon integrity led me to double down on working with him.

Sorting out teams also means putting the right person in charge and replacing people who can't contribute. In setting up a company or team, this is a lot of work and here is why. If you are sorting out a team of 10 people, you might have 5 who really belong long term on the team. It takes a while to figure out who those people are as well as who should lead and who should go. This work can be harsh. Over time, however, the percentage of people who should be on the team should be a lot more stable.

·········· 10 ··········

BUILD GREAT TEAMS, CULTIVATE MULTIPLE LEADERS

NOTHING IN BUSINESS gets done without great teams. In a small business, you need a handful of great team members. In a larger firm, you need a certain number of great team members who lead a lot of other great people. There is almost nothing more important than building out these team members and teams. With great teammates and teams, businesses can succeed in many different areas. Without great teams, business success is very limited.

Great companies need multiple great leaders. A great company has many A+ leaders. Companies that are very limited might have one great leader who has not cultivated other great leaders.

A great leader has excelled when he or she has cultivated many leaders who are more capable than he or she is. In fact, we know of organizations where leaders are assessed and measured not just based on their business results but also based on their ability to develop other successful leaders. This makes building great teams and developing more leaders part of the organization's culture.

Having leadership depth is so important because truly successful teams and organizations have great leaders throughout the organization in all functions and at all levels. As a leader, you and your teams will do far better if you can help other managers and leaders develop and thrive.

In our law practice, the worst scenario was having only one great leader. Early on in business, I recall having a very key person resign. The top lesson I took away from this experience is that if you want to build a business you ultimately need a big enough team and business so you are not overly dependent on any one person or any one customer. I used to judge the impact of a resignation by how much of a stomachache I would get. As we built a stronger team, those stomach aches decreased.

Over time, the practice really thrived as many great leaders developed. Lawyers and leaders like Amber Walsh, Holly Buckley, Bart Walker, Melissa Szabad, Geoff Cockrell, Kirsten Doell, David Pivnick, Anna Timmerman, Tim Fry, Helen Suh, Gretchen Townshend, and several more were instrumental to the practice's success.

• • • • • • • • • • • • • • • • • • • •

"I am convinced that nothing we do is more important than hiring and developing people. At the end of the day, you bet on people, not on strategies."
— Lawrence Bossidy, Former Chairman and CEO,
AlliedSignal[13]

• • • • • • • • • • • • • • • • • • • •

---

13 Noel M. Tichy and Ram Charan, "The CEO as Coach: An Interview with AlliedSignal's Lawrence A. Bossidy," *Harvard Business Review*, March–April 1995. https://hbr. org/1995/03/the-ceo-as-coach-an-interview-with-alliedsignals-lawrence-a-bossidy.

············ **11** ············

SORTING OUT PEOPLE AND TEAMS

AS A BUSINESS leader, it is very difficult work to make difficult choices and sort out people and teams. If a team is going to thrive, it needs hard-working, talented people. When building out any kind of team, it's challenging to sort out and build something largely composed of high-value contributors. This is an absolute necessity in business and if done right, it provides the foundation for long-term success. If not done well, it's often a prescription for long-term mediocrity.

When we discuss sorting out teams, particularly early on this often means identifying who can lead, who can be a key part of the team, and who does not belong. This "sorting" people out is no fun, but in my experience, it is critical to building great firms and teams.

I have found the "33% Rule" to be helpful—it's an inexact rule, but I've found it to be true in companies of many sizes. Here is the concept. Some percent of your teams and leaders need to be long term and viewed as almost indispensable. Some percentage is very, very important. And some can turn over with little concern—it's no fun, but not a big deal. The top 33% you do everything you can to keep thriving.

With the 33% Rule in mind, it's also crucial to remember that great people are keepers. At one point 15 years ago, before remote work was a thing, some of our best colleagues—Melissa Szabad and Amber Walsh—had family reasons that led them to move out of Chicago. By this time, I had learned that the best people are keepers. We worked with them to stay with the firm. Each ultimately did so and each became partners with the firm. Amber became chair of the healthcare department and later a leader on the firm's executive committee. Melissa is now general counsel of a great company.

11 ESSENTIALS FOR ATTRACTING, ENGAGING, AND RETAINING THE BEST PEOPLE

GALLUP'S STATE OF the Global Workplace: 2023 Report found that over two-thirds of employees in the United States and Canada are either not engaged (52%) or are actively disengaged (17%).[14]

We have found that the following 11 essentials can help in attracting the best people and engaging them:

1. *Ensure that all jobs include some easy wins.* If every part of the job is very hard work, it's very difficult to stay with it for the long run. It's too much of a prescription for burnout.

---

14 Gallup State of the Global Workforce: 2023 Report. https://www.gallup.com/workplace/349484/state-of-the-global-workplace.aspx#ite-506924.

2. *Eliminate friction points.* Bosses and leaders must take away hurdles to completing the job wherever possible. Make it easy for people to do their job.

3. *Make the results of one's work apparent.* It is satisfying and good for morale to see your work clearly making a difference and helping the team or company progress.

4. *Measure performance based on results.* Performance should not be based on hours or excessive oversight. The quantity and quality of work required must be rational both to the person who is doing the job and to the needs of the company and its customers.

5. *Allow people to pursue growth.* There should be the opportunity to take on different challenges and opportunities within the job. Growth is essential to helping employees feel like they are valued and receiving value of their own from their jobs. Staying stagnant is never positive for anyone.

. . . .

"Train people well enough so they can leave, treat them well enough so they don't want to."
  – Sir Richard Branson, Founder of The Virgin Group[15]

. . . .

---

15 "In a Few Words Richard Branson Gave a Priceless Lesson on What Separates Great Leaders From the Pack," Marcel Schwantes, Inc., March 14, 2023. https://www.inc.com/marcel-schwantes/in-a-few-words-sir-richard-branson-gave-a-priceless-lesson-on-what-separates-great-leaders-from-pack.html.

6. *Give people time to grow.* The job can't be so all-consuming that no energy is left to pursue growth opportunities within the job. Coupled with number five and number one above, this concept urges roles that allow employees to feel like they are growing.

7. *Include some flexibility in the job.* If there are quotas and other requirements, there must be room for them to be missed periodically or time to take breaks. No one likes to feel constantly policed or like Big Brother is constantly looking over their shoulders.

8. *Reward people who exceed the core job.* Recognize those who have gone above and beyond and have made a significant contribution.

9. *Provide pathways for growth and promotion.* Again, staying stagnant is terrible for all parties.

10. *Look for ways to work more efficiently.* The goal is to make jobs easier without sacrificing quality.

11. *Focus on the culture.* The business culture must include both nice people and a culture of appreciation.

. . . .

"Fully engaged employees are dedicated to an organization's purpose, certain in their definition of excellence, confident in the support of their teammates, and excited by their organization's future."
– Marcus Buckingham, Head of Research,
People + Performance, ADP Research Institute[16]

. . . .

---

16 Marcus Buckingham, "The Top 10 Findings on Resilience and Engagement," *MIT Sloan Management Review*, March 1, 2021. https://sloanreview.mit.edu/article/the-top-10-findings-on-resilience-and-engagement/.

YOUR BEST PEOPLE WILL HAVE UPS AND DOWNS

IF YOU ARE going to work with people over sustained periods of time, it's critical that you understand that everyone will have ups and downs, just as we do.

As a leader, it's important to give all of your people grace and room during challenging times and to provide understanding during those times.

As you grow in business, over time you learn how important your very best people are. Then you also learn that they will go through periods of time where their performance can be distracted. I recall when one of my very best colleagues lost his wife to cancer. It took a couple of years for him to really get back to focus at work and perform as he always had. These periods of time when people have life events that get in the way of work happen in many different ways and they happen at some point or another to all of us. Personally, I have gone through periods of time where my work efforts weren't at their best. It's crucial to learn to value people as long-term contributors and key team members and to be patient through the tough times. Great people are very hard to find. Keep them through good and bad times.

. . . .

"Forgiveness is not an occasional act; it is a constant attitude."

– Martin Luther King, Jr.[17]

. . . .

17 Martin Luther King, Jr., Draft of Chapter IV, "Love in Action," The King Papers – The Martin Luther King, Jr. Research and Education Institute, Stanford University. https://kinginstitute.stanford.edu/king-papers/documents/draft-chapter-iv-love-action.

········· **14** ·········

RECRUIT, RETAIN, AND AUTOMATE

THE GREAT GAME in business today is twofold:

1. *Recruit and retain great people.* There is an increased premium today on retaining and recruiting great people. More and more, these people are overseeing the bigger, more important tasks in firms. They are interacting with customers, assessing what the products look like, working with outsourced resources, and taking care of a wide mix of responsibilities.

2. *Automate every function where there is a return on investment.* Automation is valuable when it eliminates burdens for the workforce, generates greater efficiencies, and supports higher levels of customer service. We encourage a constant focus on what can be automated and what can be outsourced effectively.

11 THOUGHTS ON HIRING, PROMOTION, AND RETENTION

TO BUILD GREAT teams, leaders must focus on every phase of the employee lifecycle, from hiring new talent to developing their skills and creating a culture that makes people want to stay in the organization.

One other concept we talk about with regard to hiring is being willing to hire people better and smarter than yourself and to encourage your managers to do so. The great business author Jeff Fox often says you want to avoid having "7s hire 5s." In contrast, you want to encourage your leaders to embrace hiring the best people possible, particularly people more capable than themselves.

Here are 11 thoughts on hiring, promotion, and retention based on my experience:

1. *Give employees time to show what they're made of.* You don't really know what you have until someone has worked with you for some period of time. I can't tell you how many times someone has pointed to a hire and thought that person would be fantastic and then they were not. In contrast, the same thing happens on the other side. A person is hired and expectations are fine and then they end up being a total leader.

2. *Hire based on a mix of characteristics.* I often err toward candidates with great grades, statistics, prior performance, and evidence that they don't job hop. Regardless of the characteristics you focus on, hiring is an educated guess and a gamble. You don't really know what you have until someone works with you closely for some time.

3. *Don't judge your hires too early.* Avoid judging your hires until you and your team have worked with them for some time. I recall three partners joining us a long time ago in a particular area. All seemed solid for a couple of years. One constantly demonstrated a different level of energy, effort, and insight. Over time, that individual become a complete leader. It was critical not to prejudge those three colleagues. All were solid performers, but one ended up unbelievable.

4. *Proactively reward strong performers.* When someone starts to show the drive, contribution, and efforts you want, constantly encourage, support, promote, and pay them. Don't wait until they push you for what they deserve. Get out in front of it. A few of my best colleagues showed such clear promise early on that we kept looking to put them in charge of more and more, even when others weren't so sure. These were some of the best business decisions I ever made.

5. *Don't hire people on the cheap.* Even when you can hire people cheaply, don't do it. Pay a salary or amount where the person won't wake up every morning feeling irritated at the firm.

6. *Remember that you will occasionally have to end business relationships.* When someone demonstrates on a consistent basis that they can't or won't do the job, you probably need to ask them nicely to go or to start looking for a new job. I tried very hard over the years to do this with as little harm to the person as possible.

7. *Give your best colleagues the best assignments.* The best performers tend to get the best opportunities and assignments. Don't apologize for putting your best colleagues on the most important client accounts and in the most important roles.

8. *Don't promote as a way to change performance.* Promoting someone into a title won't change the way they act or perform.

9. *Reward people who are already performing at a higher level.* The best promotions go to those who already act like they are doing a higher level job. A partnership or VP promotion is simple when a colleague is already performing at that level.

10. *Don't punish leaders for the occasional bad hire.* We all need to understand that hiring is an educated guess and an imperfect process. You can't allow your leaders to become too gun shy regarding hiring due to the periodic bad hiring decision.

11. *Offer people the opportunity to find a role that fits.* If people are great individuals, but they aren't excelling in their roles, try them in other roles. Some of our best colleagues changed roles a few times internally before they excelled.

······· *Section 3* ·······

DO YOU HAVE WHAT IT TAKES?

·············

BECOMING A GREAT LEADER

······························

BECOMING A GREAT LEADER
(CHAPTERS 16–20)

Great leaders have a bias toward action and urgency. In addition, they create an environment where team members can thrive—that means cultivating a culture that is human, performance-driven, grateful, mission-driven, authentic, and open.

Great leaders understand the importance of hiring great people and then giving them room to thrive. They encourage experimentation and learning while accepting the occasional failure as an important way to learn.

·········· **16** ··········

THE FOUNDER'S EVOLUTION IN THREE STAGES

THERE ARE COUNTLESS stages in developing a business. These can include the idea, the first customer, the first employee, the first profit, the first crisis, the exit, and so many more.

In our experience, we have found that founders and anyone building a team of any sort encounter the following three stages:

- *Stage 1: Formation.* This stage generally involves the founder having an idea and largely being a one-person show. Here, the founder is salesperson, execution person, customer person, billing person, and a whole lot more. Over time, the founder will outsource some of the functions, but he or she is still running a relatively limited and small business. He or she, for all practical purposes, handles most roles.

- *Stage 2: Build-Out.* During this stage, the founder starts to hire full-time employees. Typically, the founder largely hires people who are handling different roles but are not necessarily more talented than the founder. Rather, they are allowing the founder to do more of what the founder is great at, but they are not really expanding the business beyond the game plan or vision of the founder. This is often a better model than in the first stage, but it is still limits how far the business can go. Generally, the business is still living in a box, albeit a bigger box and hopefully a more impactful box.

- *Stage 3: Scaling.* In this stage of a business, the founder has built a team where almost every function is now handled by a person who is better at that function than the founder. For example, the chief commercial officer can build and sell in a way the founder could not. The chief product officer can evolve products that are better than the founder could. The chief people officer can build a team and grow a team better than the founder could. As a result, the business no longer lives in a box. It's in this area that great businesses can start to grow and scale.

········· **17** ·········

ANALYZING VS. ACTING IN MANAGEMENT AND BUSINESS

IN MANAGEMENT, A bias for action is critical to success and to learning. Ultimately, to make progress one needs to be working at something and trying to constantly learn while doing. There is a ton written on how activity and busyness are not the key to success. While balance and not overextending yourself are important, it's also critical to have a bias for action and a sense of urgency coupled with thought and analysis. Many people and businesses get paralyzed by too much analysis.

For years, I dawdled on how to develop the Becker Private Equity and Business Podcast. Once I stopped dawdling, focused on a few key decisions, and acted on those, the podcast rose quickly—often reaching the top of the Apple Business News charts. It took making clear decisions and acting on them.

A second example is when Jessica Cole—the president and CEO of Becker's Healthcare—would often say that salespeople come in two types. The first are those who aim 20 times and then maybe fire, and the second are those who take aim and fire. We prefer the second type. In any event, great leaders need to be able to make many decisions and a good percentage of them must be correct, then they need to execute on them.

. . . .

"It's not about ideas. It's about making ideas happen."
– Scott Belsky, Chief Strategy Officer,
Executive Vice President of Design &
Emerging Products, Adobe[18]

. . . .

---

18 Scott Belsky. https://www.scottbelsky.com/.

········· **18** ·········

GRATEFUL AND HIGH PRAISE, NO BLAME CULTURES

WE BELIEVE THE phrase "thank you" and the constant showing of gratitude is critical to building a great culture. We also believe that if someone is largely doing their job well, the manager should strive to applaud the greatness and largely ignore the imperfections. Focus heavily on the positive. Don't nitpick the negative.

························

"When it comes to life, the critical thing is whether you take things for granted or take them with gratitude."
– G.K. Chesterton, Writer & Philosopher[19]

························

It's worth taking a moment to discuss company and business culture. The concept of culture has become much more

---

19   Sarah Lemire and Barbara Bellesi Zito, "68 gratitude quotes to express your deep appreciation this year," Today, November 21, 2023. https://www.today.com/life/quotes/gratitude-quotes-rcna40290.

pronounced over the years. There are multiple ways to consider culture. Here are three that we think are important:

1. *Be a firm or company that people want to work at.* It can't be a top-down culture where people are treated like machine parts.

2. *Be mission-driven.* Your culture must be focused on achieving the firm's mission.

3. *Be authentic.* You can't build a culture that is not reflective of your real thoughts and beliefs.

In the law firm setting and in business in general, one of the best pieces of advice I ever received came from a young lawyer at the time named Marcelo Corpuz. At that time, I was a young manager, and periodically I would yell at or berate a colleague to try and get things done better. Marcelo had the gumption to pull me aside and say, whether I was right or wrong about the quality of work, that my manner of motivating or trying to get things done was killing the culture of the team. Yelling and berating may work short term, but longer term it's detrimental as a method of management.

Certain leaders like Marion and William Crawford, as well as Jim Carroll, Marc Benjamin, Brian Levy, Andy Friedman, Marc Blum, Jim Keller, Jim Field, and David Stafman, provide great examples of building positive cultures.

. . . .

"Culture is the unique way that your organization lives out its company purpose and delivers on its brand promise to customers. For this reason, a strong corporate culture functions as a differentiator in the marketplace."

– Gallup[20]

. . . .

---

20 "What Is Organizational Culture? And Why Does It Matter?" Gallup. https://www. gallup.com/workplace/327371/how-to-build-better-company-culture.aspx#ite-327398.

FAILURE IS FINE ... WITHIN REASON

YOU WANT TO grow team members and leaders who are not afraid to periodically fail. While you don't want failure to become a habit, you do want people to be willing to try new areas, new business lines, and new roles and know that as long as they give it a great effort, they will not be forever judged on periodic failures. We want people brave enough and confident enough to withstand some setbacks. Some of the best learning comes from failing.

Some of the best people on our teams, whether in the law firm or media business, really thrived in their second or third position at the company. They showed enough of the right attitude, efforts, and competence to make it clear we wanted them with the firm forever but needed to find the right spot for them.

To create a work environment where failure is accepted, you must promote a culture where people feel comfortable experimenting and taking reasonable risks. The best failures happen quickly, inexpensively, and serve as valuable learning experiences.

· · · · · · · · · · · · · · · · · · · ·

"I have not failed. I've just found 10,000 ways that won't work."

– Thomas Edison[21]

· · · · · · · · · · · · · · · · · · · ·

21 "The Importance of Thomas Edison's Quotes," The Edison Innovation Foundation. https://www.thomasedison.org/edison-quotes.

THREE KEYS TO JUDGING LEADERS

1. *Results are critical.* There is no getting around judging a leader based on his or her team's performance or the company's performance. Identify the organization's core objectives and evaluate whether the team, leader, and company are meeting those objectives.

2. *Developing more leaders is essential.* A leader should be judged on how many outstanding leaders and team members he or she develop, grows, and helps to cultivate. A leader who delivers results but doesn't fully grow a team and other leaders will generate results that are aren't sustainable for the organization.

3. *Ask what the organization looks like when the leader stops leading.* For example, perhaps the greatest compliment to the leadership of Steve Jobs or Bill Gates is how Apple and Microsoft have thrived after their leadership period ended.

While I'm proud of some efforts and not so proud of others, one key thing I take pride in is the number of people who have become leaders and thrived under my leadership. Here my trick wasn't being great at training others. I'd say I was fine, but I don't have the temperament to always be a great trainer. Rather my strength was seeing the qualities in others that made them great and often doubling down on those people with coaching, promotions, and raises very early on. That helped those people thrive with us and side-by-side.

The effort to see potential and greatness in others and not worrying about compensation or promotion rules was my strength in developing, keeping, and growing leaders. They did the hard work. My strength was seeing it in them and doubling down.

• • • • • • • • • • • • • • • • • • • •

"Before you are a leader, success is all about growing yourself. When you become a leader, success is all about growing others."

– Jack Welch, Winning[22]

• • • • • • • • • • • • • • • • • • • •

---

22 "3 Tips for Being a Truly Great Leader," Fortune. https://fortune.com/2016/11/16/xerox-key-to-great-leadership/#:~:text=Great%20leaders%20don't%20just,is%20all%20about%20growing%20others.%E2%80%9D.

······· *Section 4* ·······

CAN YOU GET FROM HERE TO THERE?

············

SCALING A BUSINESS

·····································

SCALING A BUSINESS (CHAPTERS 21-29)

Once a business is up and running, making it a continuing success requires action on several fronts. In our experience, leaders must engage in an ongoing review of the fundamentals of the business.

They engage in learning and experimenting by taking a lot of small shots, defining clear priorities, and constantly setting achievable goals. Having a laser focus on what your organization does best and then outsourcing the rest is another important part of scaling a business.

For me, finding the motivation to build bigger businesses came from several different spots. Early on, I wanted to attain some level of financial and business independence—I had watched how beholden lawyers were at my initial firm to rainmakers if they didn't have some control over their business. I never wanted to treat people how those colleagues were treated, but I was also very anxious not to be in that position myself.

Another source of motivation came from watching my dad who did amazing work for a large company and then that company went bankrupt. My father was their first million-dollar salesperson, but that didn't matter once the company that my father worked for went broke. My parents, Naomi and Mort Becker, showed tremendous resilience and dedication to business and to their children. An amazing set of leaders and parents. My mother, like Mady Elman, is a generational matriarch.

Later, my motivation came from necessity. As we talk about

often, business success is all about building great teams. Here, my CEO Jessica Cole decided about 20 years ago that we couldn't have the team we wanted without building a bigger business to provide the level of opportunities needed for our people.

With all that said, we view that there are five stages in growing a business. One can view this as a funnel where many aspiring entrepreneurs start in stage one and a lot fewer make it to stage four or five.

- *Stage 1.* The entrepreneur or investor has an idea.
- *Stage 2.* That idea actually becomes a service or a product.
- *Stage 3.* The company starts to generate revenues.
- *Stage 4.* The company can take the next step and make a profit from those revenues and products and services.
- *Stage 5.* The company scales and grows to a whole different level and size.

This section provides lessons for all five stages, especially entrepreneurs trying to get to Stage 5.

········· **21** ·········

YOU NEED TO UNDERSTAND YOUR OWN BUSINESS!

EVERY LEADER SHOULD understand very clearly where their revenues and profits are coming from, who their best people are, and what their competition looks like. The leader should be so engaged that he or she can see the business clearly as well as the pivots that need to be made.

A key to business success is to double down on the places and clients where revenues and profits come from and to double down on key leaders and key people.

Before looking at new ideas, big global trends, or other concepts, we encourage people to first fully understand their own business by engaging in regular self-assessments. By regular, we recommend at least annually.

During a self-assessment, ask several questions including:

1. Where do your revenues and profits come from?
2. Who are your key customers and who are their core teams and people?
3. Should you pour more resources into your key customers and markets or expand and look at new areas?

In our various experiences, we have found that leaders who really know their business, their own firm, and their customers are the best leaders.

We have seen a few quotes that illustrate the importance of understanding your business and your customers. Amazon founder Jeff Bezos has said, "If you don't understand the details of your business, you are going to fail."[23] Dave Thomas, the founder of Wendy's, was quoted as saying, "What do you need to start a business? Three simple things: know your product better than anyone, know your customer, and have a burning desire to succeed."[24]

---

23 Darren DeMatas, "40 Entrepreneur Quotes to Spark Motivation and Success," ecommerceCEO, June 6, 2023. https://www.ecommerceceo.com/entrepreneur-quotes-for-motivation/.

24 Craig Bloem, "Founder of Wendy's Dave Thomas Says You Need These 3 Things to Start a Business," Inc.com, April 25, 2019. https://www.inc.com/craig-bloem/wendys-founder-dave-thomas-said-you-need-3-things-to-start-a-business-here-are-mine.html.

HOW TO GROW A COMPANY— ORGANIC GROWTH VS. MERGERS AND ACQUISITIONS

MOST COMPANIES NEED a mix of two types of growth to thrive in the long run:

- *Organic growth.* This results from generating more revenue and profits through the company's existing products and services. It can mean selling more to existing customers, targeting new groups of customers and new channels, and developing innovative new products and services. Organic growth is often based on having clear goals, effective processes, and executing with excellence. In our experience, for most companies sustained organic growth is a key "engine" to enduring success.

- *Acquisition growth.* In a company's early stages, most growth will be organic, but as a company gets larger, a merger or an acquisition can be an important way to grow. Acquisitions can jumpstart growth by gaining access to new teams, products, customers, channels, or technologies. A sign of an unhealthy company, however, is a company that overly relies heavily on acquisitions to fuel growth while not maintaining strong internal operations.

• • • • • • • • • • • • • • • • • • • •

"From time to time it's important to highlight the acquisition strategies being used in the M&A market right now... One such strategy you need to be aware of is the current evolution in the growth of add-on acquisitions by Private Equity Firms (PE) to platform holdings. This tactical growth plan is used by PE firms post-acquisition of an initial "platform" company; over the course of several years, smaller, very targeted acquisitions are made that complement the platform, allowing it to expand much faster than it would organically.

This strategy allows the PE firm to gradually build a much larger entity and, using various economies of scale, reach new levels of revenue and profit that would be hard to achieve without the add-on program in place."

– Generational Equity[25]

• • • • • • • • • • • • • • • • • • • •

---

25 "Why Do PE Firms Use Add-On Acquisitions to Grow?" Generational Equity. https://www.genequityco.com.

········· **23** ·········

PIVOTS ARE THE NORM

IN EVERY BUSINESS, a founder or leader develops a plan and a team. Over time, with both plans and people one will almost always need to make changes or what we call pivots. It's normal to start with a plan and then make adjustments as you gain experience and as circumstances change.

Several of the bigger pivots we made at the law firm included the following:

- The pivot from service lawyer to business-generating lawyer

- The pivot from general business lawyer to lawyer serving healthcare clients

- The pivot from a focus on several areas to focusing almost exclusively on surgery centers, health systems, and private equity funds

In the healthcare media business, we were originally just in print and focused on the surgery center market. There we had to pivot from print to digital and from simply surgery centers to surgery centers, health systems, and orthopedics and spine. Health systems has become our biggest area by far.

From a more general business leadership perspective, we had to pivot from me being in charge to handing over leadership to people who could grow the business in a whole different way than I could.

As the boxer Mike Tyson has famously said, "Everyone has a plan until they get punched in the mouth." In our experience, you don't need to get punched in the mouth to see the need to pivot, you just need to be open-minded in seeing that there is a different and better way to do things.

Usually, pivots are adjustments versus wholesale changes, and generally they are closer to the core versus complete changes. Overall, a business leader must both focus on their core business and be open to making changes.

According to Rory M. McDonald, associate professor at Harvard Business School, sooner or later every successful company will have to make a pivot. That might be adapting its product, moving into a more promising market, or adjusting to a changing business environment. Whatever the circumstance, organizations must maintain trust and project their original vision during the process of pivoting. Leaders must explain how their new plan ties to the original vision.[26]

. . . .

"A pivot is a change in strategy without a change in vision."

– Eric Ries, author of The Lean Startup[27]

. . . .

26 Lane Lambert, "8 Strategies to Sustain Business Innovation," HBS Working Knowledge, September 23, 2022. https://hbswk.hbs.edu/item/book-productive-tensions-how-every-leader-can-tackle-innovations-toughest-trade-offs-rory-mcdonald.

27 Nikki Carlson, "How Companies Are Learning To Pivot In The Current Business Environment," Forbes, May 15, 2020. https://www.forbes.com/sites/theyec/2020/05/15/how-companies-are-learning-to-pivot-in-the-current-business-environment/?sh=4f3a70d827ae.

········· **24** ·········

TAKE SHOTS AT THE PLATE

IT IS CRITICAL that while knowing and sticking to your core, you frequently take chances and "shots at the plate." Taking frequent low-risk shots is the best way to learn, grow, and identify exciting new opportunities.

·····················
"You miss 100% of the shots you don't take."
– Wayne Gretzky[28]
·····················

Here, we believe in the concept of regularly taking measured risks and the concept promulgated by author and speaker Jim Collins. When it comes to testing things, he says, "Fire bullets, not cannons!" This concept ties closely to the idea that some mistakes and failures are fine, but there is a need to ensure measured failures and challenges.

---

28 Ryan Glasspiegel, "Wayne Gretzky pays homage to Michael Scott's famous stolen 'Office' quote," New York Post, May 6, 2022. https://nypost.com/2022/05/06/wayne-gretzky-pays-homage-to-michael-scotts-stolen-quote/.

Success often results from seeing opportunities that sometimes hit you in the face and doubling down on them hard core. When you see great opportunities or great people, you need to be willing to invest behind them with your time and money.

This was true for me with great people and seeing chances to build a healthcare legal practice, invest in surgery centers with great managers, and doubling and tripling down on building a great media company. So much of this is making the effort to see what is in front of you and being willing to go after it when you see it.

······· **25** ········

FOCUS ON CORE COMPETENCIES; OUTSOURCE EVERYTHING ELSE

IN WHATEVER BUSINESS you are in, you want to decide what your core competencies are and what you need to be great at to be successful. Then, you want to figure out how to stack your teams and resources around those core competencies and outsource everything else.

·····················
"Do what you do best and outsource the rest."
                        – Peter Drucker[29]
·····················

In originally building our media business, we had a very small team and had to decide where we wanted to build out and focus our own internal teams and where it would be better to outsource. We originally decided that we wanted to build our own teams

---

29 "A New Way to Outsource," Forbes, June 1, 2010. https://www.forbes.com/2010/06/01/vested-outsourcing-microsoft-intel-leadership-managing-kate-vitasek.html?sh=b3d601567363 .

and expertise around editorial, sales, conferences, and key account management. It was much easier and more effective to build teams around a handful of areas rather than trying to be great in everything.

Over time, a few more areas became areas that we defined as core competencies. We had to be great in data and analytics and in distribution. As a growing company, you need to decide what you have to be great in and what is critical to your business.

Don't take outsourcing for granted. It's serious work to find and cultivate great outsourcing partners. Finding great partners that you trust will simplify the lives of your employees and will allow them to focus on the most important things. In the media business, for example, we initially tried outsourcing some writing to India, but this didn't work because we didn't have good enough processes in place to ensure strict quality control. When you outsource, you have to devote time to managing your outsourced partners and hold them accountable. But outsourcing, if done right in the right parts of your business, can greatly improve service to customers and the organization's scalability.

A successful business has identified what it can do better than anyone else and why. Its core competencies are the "why." Core competencies are also known as core capabilities or distinctive competencies. Core competencies lead to competitive advantages.

In their 1990 *Harvard Business Review* article, "The Core Competence of the Corporation," C.K. Prahalad and Gary Hamel reviewed three conditions that a business activity must meet to be a core competency:

1. The activity must provide superior value or benefits to the consumer.
2. It should be difficult for a competitor to replicate or imitate it.
3. It should be rare.[30]

---

30 Alexandra Twin, "Core Competencies in Business: Finding a Competitive Advantage," Investopedia, August 30, 2023. https://www.investopedia.com/terms/c/core_competencies.asp.

SIMPLICITY IS THE NAME OF THE GAME

THE SIMPLER YOU and your firm make production and the simpler you define your core product and value to customers, for example, the easier it is to get things done and get everyone on the same page. Simplicity reduces friction in the workplace and in processes. One of the worst phrases in business is, "We have always done it this way." If a meeting can be done in 5 minutes, not 30, do it in 5. The story is the same everywhere—always look to simplify.

Simplicity in everything is critical. In writing a memo to a client, aim for shorter versus longer—provide summaries, not extensive and unnecessary details. In developing a team and organization, work to focus on the absolute key areas that you need to be great in and outsource everything else. In defining what your firm needs to excel, aim to clarify and simplify as much as possible.

At Becker's Healthcare, we moved to an editorial version nearly 20 years ago that most, if not all, writing had to be short-form journalism. This made it easier for our journalists to write the articles, easier for our editors to edit the articles, and very importantly, easier for our readers to read the articles. Similarly, we tended to move toward shorter panelist sessions at conferences. We learned to outsource to BullsEye Resources what we could intelligently outsource.

At the law firm, we learned that all client communications should have a one-page summary so the client could immediately see the key issues or findings. We also moved to constant, short, simple meetings with essentially the same key agenda points to help align everyone on the same page and make sure that things get done as they should be.

Mark Twain famously wrote, "I would have written a shorter letter, but I didn't have the time." Moving to simplicity pays huge dividends, but it takes work and discipline.

· ·
"Simplicity is the ultimate sophistication."
– Apple's first marketing brochure[31]
· ·

---

31 Walter Isaacson, "The Real Leadership Lessons of Steve Jobs," *Harvard Business Review*, April 2012. https://hbr.org/2012/04/the-real-leadership-lessons-of-steve-jobs.

········· **27** ·········

DON'T BECOME TOO RELIANT ON ONE PERSON OR CUSTOMER

THE WORST NUMBER in business is one. A company does not want to be too reliant on any one customer, supplier, or key leader. Being too reliant on one thing or having most of your revenue coming from one customer tends to make a business fragile. The key is to both double down on that great customer, leader, or supplier and develop additional great leaders, customers, and suppliers. The answer is to both keep your great customers and add more great customers.

In every business, you go through periods of time where the business is too dependent on a single team member or a single customer. The goal is to keep that person and customer thriving and work to add great people and customers.

While you are constantly trying to become less dependent on your most valuable people and customers, you also need to recognize that there are certain people in business that you will "ride or die with" to steal a modern phrase. At one point, a colleague said we need to make ourselves less dependent on our CEO Jessica Cole. At this point, Jessica had been my colleague and the driving force behind the company for over 10 years. Here, I retorted, "You can do that after I retire." There are certain people that you have zero desire to be in business without.

THE IMPORTANCE OF SETTING KEY PRIORITIES

SETTING CORE PRIORITIES allows you to provide clarity as to where to pursue efforts, and just as importantly, as Peter Drucker would say, where not to spend time and energy.

As you set key priorities, the concept is to invest time, money, people, and energy into those few top priorities. Develop simple systems to assess how much time and effort is being allocated to those priorities and hold the team accountable to ensure they are focusing heavily on those key priorities.

Most teams, companies, and people are best off having a few key priorities rather than many. The worst advice I have often heard college counselors give is something like, "You need fifteen items on your application." Just like in business, you are far better off being deep in a few areas than shallow in a lot of areas. As you set clear priorities, you need to be great at saying no to almost everything else. This is a key discipline.

Decide what you want to be great at and focus all of your efforts on that pursuit.

• •

"The essence of strategy is choosing what not to do."
– Michael Porter[32]

• •

---

32 Joan Magretta, "Jim Collins, Meet Michael Porter," *Harvard Business Review*, December 15, 2011. https://hbr.org/2011/12/jim-collins-meet-michael-porte.

SET GOALS THAT ARE REALISTIC AND WINNABLE, NOT EGO-DRIVEN

A HUGE AMOUNT has been written on goal setting. People talk about stretch goals, BHAG (big, hairy, audacious) goals, SMART (specific, measurable, achievable, realistic, time-bound) goals, and all kinds of goals.

In contrast, there is a school of thought discussed by Kevin O'Leary on goals that I am a bigger proponent of. Here, he essentially says that in his portfolio of companies, women leaders tend to hit their goals about 95% of the time and men hit their goals closer to 65% of the time.[33]

What makes the difference? Women tend to set realistic goals—men tend to set ego-driven goals. The concept here is that it is much better to set realistic and not ego-driven goals and to

---

33 Ali Montag, " 'Shark Tank' star Kevin O'Leary: Women-run businesses make me the most money – here's why," CNBC, March 22, 2018. https://www.cnbc.com/2018/03/22/shark-tanks-kevin-oleary-women-make-me-the-most-money.html.

hit them again and again. In the long run, this leads to greater confidence, sustainability, and growth of teams.

· ·

"Make realistic goals, just keep reevaluating, and be consistent."

– Venus Williams[34]

· ·

---

34 Anna Moeslein, "What a Day in the (Very Healthy) Life of Venus Williams Is Like – Her Workout Tips, Fave Low-Cal Snacks, and More," *Glamour*, May 7, 2013. https://www.glamour.com/story/healthy-eating-and-workout-tip.

······· *Section 5* ·······

IS THIS IT??

· · · · · · · · · ·

FINDING ENDURING SUCCESS

· ·

FINDING ENDURING SUCCESS
(CHAPTERS 30-38)

One of life's great goals is to find enduring personal and professional success. I think it can be helpful to focus on four things that we say to our children:

- Physical and mental health should be lifetime priorities
- Be a constructive adult—this can apply to a wide range of areas
- Keep leaning into things that spark your interest
- Pursue passions in life and also be able to support yourself and your family

As I reflect on personal and professional success, several different concepts come to mind which are listed below and expounded upon in the following chapters.

1. Physical and mental health
2. Clarity of goals and direction
3. Learning to protect yourself by saying no
4. Running your calendar and your activity level at the right balance
5. Not listening to naysayers
6. A focus on process, habits, and structure
7. Being valuable to a few key people or clients
8. Cultivating your own passion and excitement
9. Passion plus being able to support oneself
10. Building great teams and partnerships

········· **30** ·········

AN IMPORTANT NOTE ON PHYSICAL AND MENTAL HEALTH

MAKING ONE'S PHYSICAL and mental health a top priority is foundational to everything else. When you're younger, you may take this for granted. But even when you're younger, if you let this lag too much it will have bad long-term consequences. As one ages, one sees large divergences between those that have made their health a lifetime priority and those who have not. It has a large impact both professionally and on the ability to enjoy life.

One of the mantras I live by is "active into the 80s." To me, this means focusing on keeping yourself physically and mentally active throughout your entire life. I look at people such as Stan Levy, Paul Lederer, Naomi Becker, and Fred Elman with great admiration and respect for how they keep focused on mental and physical health while in their 80s.

• • • • • • • • • • • • • • • • • • • •

"What gets measured gets managed, as the old saying goes. What I think we're not paying nearly enough attention to is the quality of life. And that's what's captured in healthspan. There's a cognitive component to that. There's obviously a physical component to that. And there's an emotional component to that. If you don't define metrics around those things, it's probably not surprising that we're not managing those things. Therefore, most of the resources and attention go to simply prolonging life, even at the expense of quality."
– Dr. Peter Attia, Author of Outlive[35]

• • • • • • • • • • • • • • • • • • • •

Each of us should be able to find role models for physical and mental health and taking care of ourselves. One of my top role models here is my mother, who diligently takes care of her health through regular preventive efforts. Prevention is much easier, more cost-effective, and healthier than treating something once it's already onset.

• • • • • • • • • • • • • • • • • • • •

"Physical fitness is not only one of the most important keys to a healthy body, it is the basis of dynamic and creative intellectual activity."
– John F. Kennedy[36]

• • • • • • • • • • • • • • • • • • • •

---

35 "Dr. Peter Attia: This Is What You Need to Do to Live Longer," Amanpour & Co., PBS, June 22, 2023. https://www.pbs.org/wnet/amanpour-and-company/video/dr-peter-attia-this-is-what-you-need-to-do-to-live-longer/.

36 Maryn Liles, "Don't Sweat It! These 101 Best Fitness and Workout Quotes Will Keep You Motivated," Parade, January 6, 2024. https://parade.com/1045407/marynliles/fitness-quotes/.

THE POWER OF SAYING NO

IT IS CRITICAL to decide what you don't want to do and which goals you don't want to pursue. This applies both personally and in making business decisions. Setting boundaries and being intentional about what you and your business want and don't want to pursue is critical.

For example, around 20 years ago at Becker's Healthcare we decided that it would be far too costly to be a leader in print publishing. We made the very intentional decision to say "no" to trying to be a leader in print publishing while saying "yes" to becoming a leader in digital publishing. This proved to be a good decision. Sometimes it is important to say "no."

In our experience, people who can't say no have a very hard time being great over prolonged periods of time.

• •

"The difference between successful people and really successful people is that really successful people say no to almost everything."

– *Warren Buffett*[37]

• •

---

37 "Warren Buffett Says This 1 Simple Habit Separates Successful People From Everyone Else," University of Louisiana Monroe. https://ulm.edu/webguide/faculty/pdf/One-Important-And-Simple-Successful-Habit.pdf.

········· **32** ·········

LEARN TO TUNE OUT THE NAYSAYERS

IN ANY EFFORT you pursue, there will be people who discourage you or believe you cannot accomplish your goals or build your business. Over time, I have found that it's critical to take a mixed approach to those people.

1. *Don't let them stop you from moving forward.* There will always be people who don't believe in you and sometimes there may be no one who does. Have the confidence to push forward, even in the face of negativity, and you will find those who support you and believe in you.

2. *Use their negativity as fuel to push you forward.* Instead of letting it ruin your mood, plans, or confidence, take it as fuel for your fire. Work hard to prove the doubters wrong.

In any pursuit I have been involved in, someone has laughed at my efforts early on or tried to dissuade me from the pursuit. Learn to ignore the naysayers.

• •

"I have found it advisable not to give too much heed to what people say when I am trying to accomplish something of consequence. Invariably they proclaim it can't be done. I deem that the very best time to make the effort."

– Calvin Coolidge[38]

• •

38 "Coolidge Administration Accomplishments," Calvin Coolidge Presidential Foundation. https://coolidgefoundation.org/presidency/coolidge-administration-accomplishments/.

········· **33** ·········

PASSION IS THE SECRET INGREDIENT

MOST OF US, throughout our careers, work through very different periods of time in terms of motivation, excitement, and passion. In certain periods, we are grabbed by a project, idea, or set of goals and find it very easy to sustain and drive energy. At other times, it feels like one has to try and manufacture that energy and drive. When we have it flowing naturally, we are far more productive and effective than when we don't. Thus, a core concept is to constantly look for ways to ignite and encourage that passion in both ourselves and others.

- -

"If you are passionate about your ideas, it's much easier to sell them to your team. Once your team has bought in, it can be even easier to motivate employees to move a project forward. In my experience, people will work harder to bring ideas to life if there is passion and excitement behind them. This momentum is what a strong business model relies on to evolve."

– Lauren Irwin-Szostak, President and CEO, Business Processes Redefined, LLC[39]

- -

- -

"If you love your work, you'll be out there every day trying to do it the best you possibly can, and pretty soon everybody around will catch the passion from you—like a fever."

– Sam Walton[40]

- -

---

39 Laure Irwin-Szostak, "How Passion Can Translate Into A Successful Business," Forbes, November 8, 2022. https://www.forbes.com/sites/forbesbusinesscouncil/2022/11/08/how-passion-can-translate-into-a-successful-business/?sh=76c37d6740dd.

40 Donald C. Kelly, "70 Quotes About Hard Work That'll Help You Reach Your Goals," HubSpot. https://blog.hubspot.com/sales/hard-work-quotes.

· · · · · · · · · · 34 · · · · · · · · ·
"I HAVE TO" VS. "I GET TO"

IN MANAGING ONESELF, it's incredibly important to constantly keep the right paradigm and perspective. One key idea is rather than saying, "I have to do something," take the view of, "I get to." It's a perspective that can make all the difference in the world in your passion and energy and how you approach things.

Instead of saying, "I have to write this post," or "I have to give this talk," turn your perspective around and think, "How lucky am I that I get to do this?" It should be a constant reminder to us all.

········· **35** ·········

DIGGING DITCHES

YOU MUST DIG 10 ditches before they start digging themselves. This concept is used to explain that in starting something like trying to build a business, one needs to generally put forth a lot of effort before the effort starts to pay off. It takes a good deal of action and forward steps before one starts to see some of the positive results from the efforts.

We use this concept to remind myself and others that it takes serious investment in an area before you start to see results. We have read numerous quotes from people who were suddenly celebrated as "an overnight success" who stated that what might have seemed like an overnight success actually took 10 or 20 or 30 years of constant and relentless effort.

In building a legal practice, I recalled earlier that in my first year of truly trying to build a practice, my clients brought in $7,000 in legal fees. Once I really got going through constantly marketing, team building, and taking care of clients, that number grew tremendously. As Jim Collins would say, we hit a flywheel. It took prolonged effort to hit that flywheel.

Similarly in the media business, I remember over 30 years ago when we had our first $10,000 client. It took a lot of years and focus to move from that to our first million-dollar clients. In every endeavor, it takes a lot of effort to really get it going.

· ·

"Pixar's seen by a lot of folks as an overnight success, but if you really look closely, most overnight successes took a long time."

– Steve Jobs[41]

· ·

41 "The Pixar Story," 2007. https://www.imdb.com/title/tt1059955/characters/
nm0423418.

········· **36** ·········

OBSESS TO WIN AND EXCEL

A CONCEPT WE think about often is the concept that for most real success, one will need to really dig into something and obsess over it for some prolonged period of time to have substantial success.

This is an uncomfortable truth in that it requires great and intelligent effort to build greatness in anything.

· ·

"Obstacles can't stop you. Problems can't stop you. Most of all, other people can't stop you. Only you can stop you."

– Jeffrey Gitomer[42]

· ·

Ben Stein has written that it takes 10 years of commitment to really build something serious. In my experience, this kind of very focused effort with full engagement was really needed in both the

---

42 Donald C. Kelly, "70 Quotes About Hard Work That'll Help You Reach Your Goals," HubSpot. https://blog.hubspot.com/sales/hard-work-quotes.

law practice and the media business. I think it's really hard to do something substantial without a prolonged, focused effort.

We are inspired by the commitment and obsession of incredibly successful athletes such as Michael Jordan and Tom Brady, whose obsession to win was legendary. A backup to Tom Brady once observed, "When I got there, I thought I worked hard, then I watched we he did and put into it, and it was on a whole different level. There's a reason he's the best there ever was."

········· **37** ·········

HOW TO TURN AROUND FROM FAILURE WHEN YOU'RE YOUNG

RECENTLY, A QUESTION was asked on a podcast by a 21-year-old who had failed multiple times as an entrepreneur. He wanted to know how to come back from these failures.

The best way to handle this is to both get a job and focus on being an entrepreneur. A job provides structure, a place to learn, stability, and a lot more. It's not an either/or situation. A job also provides a fertile place to come up with ideas. So do both—get a job, earn a paycheck, and look for ideas as an entrepreneur, too.

· ·

"Fail early, fail often, but always fail forward."
– John C. Maxwell[43]

· ·

---

43 Maxwell Leadership, "Failing Forward: How a Personal Growth Plan Helps You Make the Most of Your Mistakes," July 19, 2022. https://www.maxwellleadership.com/blog/failing-forward/.

······· **38** ·······

SET YOUR DIRECTION FOR SUCCESS AND SATISFACTION IN A PROFESSIONAL SERVICES FIRM

THE SINGLE MOST important determinant for long-term success and happiness in your career is being able to set your own direction. Are you doing what you want to do? When working at a professional services firm or company, be reasonably vocal about what you want to do, what you feel your strengths are, and where you see your career moving.

The concept here is that once you define your goals, you are much more likely to thrive. Most people that come into professional careers or any type of career are quite smart. Many people seem to enjoy themselves and get to the concept of "busy with purpose" when they define what they want from their job or career.

For me personally, after about four years of legal practice and some time out, I looked at the landscape and said, "If I want to do this, I want to be a rainmaker." Then I decided how to do it. Having that goal and clarity completely changed how I approached things. It made it a challenge, a game, and fun.

People will laugh at these numbers today, but back then, these were grinding and excited numbers. The first year of committing to rainmaking in my legal business, my clients brought in $7,000. Then it was $50,000, $200,000, and $600,000. After the fifth year, they brought in $1 million a year and several years later, revenues grew tremendously. Once I had a goal and clarity about it, the effort was hard, but also very satisfying and simple because I knew what I was trying to do.

The goal need not to be a rainmaker. It can be becoming the manager of a team, earning a paycheck so one can care for their family, being able to exercise, or becoming the very best in something. My only observation is that the more that people set their own purpose, the happier they are.

- - - - - - - - - - - - - - - - - - - -

"A person should set his goals as early as he can and devote all his energy and talent to getting there. With enough effort, he may achieve it. Or he may find something that is even more rewarding. But in the end, no matter what the outcome, he will know he has been alive."

– Walt Disney[44]

- - - - - - - - - - - - - - - - - - - -

---

44 Nina Zipkin, "16 Inspirational Quotes from Walt Disney," Entrepreneur, December 15, 2016. https://www.entrepreneur.com/leadership/16-inspirational-quotes-from-walt-disney/286080.

Section 6

SO, YOU WANT TO LIVE THE DREAM?

STARTING OUT AS A YOUNG PROFESSIONAL

STARTING OUT AS A YOUNG PROFESSIONAL (CHAPTERS 39–42)

We are frequently asked for advice from those just beginning their career or embarking on a new job in a new organization. The following chapters offer advice from our experiences for those of you at this stage of your lives and careers.

BUILDING SOMETHING GREAT REQUIRES SERIOUS COMMITMENT AND EFFORT

ONE OF THE great quotes from William Green's book *Richer, Wiser, Happier* is as follows: "You need a maniacal focus to be great at anything. Anyone who tells you that you can have everything all at once, you can't. I mean you don't become Roger Federer by not playing tennis. It has to be consuming."

This concept of serious commitment is true when building a great career or business. It will take some level of obsession. You are going to need to commit in a serious way.

One person said it will take about 10 years of serious work to build a great career or business. At many points during this period of time, it will feel like you have essentially two full-time jobs. For example, building your business plus taking care of customers. Or building your business while you straddle your full-time job.

In any event, serious success will take serious focus. For me, this meant for a prolonged period of time I focused on business and on children and essentially very little else. For a long period of time, there was no focus on guys' nights out or golf or anything but the two core pursuits of building the business and career and raising children. It was simple to clarify like this but hard work as well—and very satisfying.

A special shoutout to colleagues who have really followed the mantra to double down and build businesses, including Rick Levin, Mark and David Abramson, Stan Slovin, Howard Sutker, Nancy Temple, Lyn Wise, Anthony Scaramucci, Brett Messing, John Svolos, Eric Schloss, Eric Cooper, Rob Benun, Mark Sibul, Jeff Bergman, and Marion and William Crawford. Many have shown both tremendous focus and tremendous resilience.

· ·

"You can't have everything you want, but you can have the things that really matter to you. And thinking that way empowers you to work really hard for a really long period of time."

– Marissa Mayer[45]

· ·

---

45 Rose Hoare, "Marissa Mayer: Six life lessons from Yahoo CEO," CNN, July 19, 2012. https://www.cnn.com/2012/07/17/tech/mayer-yahoo-career-advice/index.html.

THREE TIPS FOR EMERGING PROFESSIONALS

1. *Make yourself indispensable.* You don't need to work with 30 people. It is far more important to be indispensable to a few.

2. *Over-communicate.* It is very important to over-communicate rather than under-communicate. Have a bias toward over-communication.

> *"Managers who inundate their teams with the same messages, over and over, via multiple media, need not feel bad about their persistence. In fact, this redundant communication works to get projects completed quickly, according to new research by Harvard Business School professor Tsedal B. Neeley and Northwestern University's Paul M. Leonardi and Elizabeth M. Gerber."*
> *– HBS Working Knowledge*[46]

3. *Always be learning.* Learn a lot about your own trade, about your own business, and about the business you work in. Ask questions, read, and work on figuring out how you can learn. Constant small learning is great. Read the newspaper but focus on gaining deep knowledge in your area rather than shallow knowledge of a variety of subjects.

Many people misunderstand the advice from their firms, which they often hear as "work for lots of different people and lots of different clients." In reality, people tend to do much better if they focus heavily on really doing great work and becoming indispensable to a few clients and colleagues.

Being worth a little bit to a lot of people or clients is bad advice. Similarly in building a business, you want to find a way to be valuable to your customers and then figure out how to duplicate or scale this.

---

46 Kim Gerard, "It's Not Nagging: Why Persistent, Redundant Communication Works," HBS Working Knowledge, April 18, 2011. https://hbswk.hbs.edu/item/its-not-nagging-why-persistent-redundant-communication-works.

CAREER ADVICE FOR YOUR FIRST JOB

STARTING A NEW job or your professional career can be as daunting as it is exciting. When entering this new territory, it's helpful to know where your energy is best focused.

- *80–90% of your effort should be in excelling at this first position.* Spend your time learning, growing, and proving your value to your new company.

······················

"If you are not willing to learn, no one can help you. If you are determined to learn, no one can stop you."
– Zig Ziglar[47]

······················

- *10–20% of your effort should be analyzing different opportunities.* Spend time seeing what others in your field are doing and stepping out of the box to see how you can

---

47 Goodreads. https://www.goodreads.com/quotes/1254382-if-you-are-not-willing-to-learn-no-one-can.

improve what you're doing. Use this to make a long-term plan for your career and future.

When it's time to look into moving into a new role, search first internally. Look around at your company and see who is thriving and who you want to be like, then look for positions open similar to theirs or in the same department.

Many young professionals spend too much time focusing on finding their next job. Here, people grow a lot more if they dig more fully into their first job and then end up getting more responsibility and more mentorship. We push people to try and commit hardcore to doing great work in their current job.

· ·

"Someone with a growth mindset views intelligence, abilities, and talents as learnable and capable of improvement through effort. On the other hand, someone with a fixed mindset views those same traits as inherently stable and unchangeable over time."
– Harvard Business School Online[48]

· ·

---

48 Catherine Cote, "Growth Mindset vs. Fixed Mindset: What's the Difference," Harvard Business School Online. https://online.hbs.edu/blog/post/growth-mindset-vs-fixed-mindset.

········· **42** ·········

COACHABILITY, COMMITMENT, AND CAREER SUCCESS

MOST LEADERS AND coaches will devote disproportionately more time to those professionals, students, or team members who are committed to their careers. Coaches and leaders can generally sense a person's level of seriousness and interest and seek cues subconsciously or otherwise as to commitment and interest. As a professional, one must demonstrate a certain level of commitment and interest if one wants to excel professionally. A professional may also "fake it till they make it" and find that level of commitment. Ultimately, of course, a professional who can't find that excitement or commitment is not likely to be highly successful in their career.

One of the things we have found is that managers and leaders spend much more time with those people who show commitment and who are really trying, particularly if those people also show competence. Like an 80-20 rule, most opportunities go to the

20% of people who have commitment, interest, and competence. We found this constantly throughout our careers in business.

• •

"Coachable people willingly accept the notion that what they perceive themselves as saying or doing could be different than actual reality. Moreover, they accept the fact that until the perception of others changes, progress hasn't been made.

By contrast, non-coachable people insist that they know exactly what they say and do at all times. In their minds, perception always matches reality. Moreover, if others' perception doesn't conform, they will say 'I changed my behavior. If they don't see it, that's on them.'"

– Jathan Janove, J.D.[49]

• •

49 Jathan Janove, J.D., "Hire for Coachability," SHRM, January 26, 2022. https://www.shrm.org/executive-network/insights/hire-coachability.

.... *Section 7* ....

BUT HOW DO YOU BUILD REAL WEALTH?

....

BECOMING A GREAT INVESTOR

....

BECOMING A GREAT INVESTOR
(CHAPTERS 43–53)

In the other sections of this book, we've shared lessons in areas like entrepreneurship, leadership, and getting started in one's career. An important area that is too often overlooked by people of all ages is the importance of investing over the long term to build wealth.

The chapters that follow share practical information that we've learned over the course of our lives and careers about the basics of investing. Key lessons include being clear about your investment goals and motivations, deciding how much to invest, how best to allocate your investments, understanding your investments, and important considerations related to stocks, bonds, other types of investments, and more.

In reading this section, please note that I have used these concepts to solely manage our own family wealth and investments. I am not a registered investment advisor nor do I manage anyone else's money. I have learned a lot, but seek the advice of true investment professionals. My luck with them has been all over the board. As a result, I have gravitated back to managing our money via a small family office where we use many of the concepts discussed in this book. We have a clear plan and goals and like to work with the right people.

FIVE PIECES OF ADVICE FOR THE NEW INVESTOR

HERE ARE FIVE insights that may be helpful for new investors:

1. *Put away as much money as you can as often as you can.* Aiming to save and invest 10% to 20% of your annual income is a good rule of thumb. Keep your spending under enough control so that you can do this largely every month and every year.

2. *Max out on your employer-offered retirement plan.* This allows you to put money away and have the assets and funds grow over time in a tax-deferred manner. Make sure you are still saving money outside of these accounts that you can use in an emergency.

3. *Find a core index fund to invest in.* An S&P 500 or Vanguard S&P 500 Index Fund are great options. Put the

core of your portfolio in a broad index fund and keep a smaller percent into things you want to explore.

4. *Know your allocations.* This is the percentage of your investments allocated to equities, bonds, and cash. As a starting investor, you will probably skew toward a high equity concentration since you're investing for long-term growth. As you get older, you might diversify your allocations for safety.

5. *Don't stress out day-to-day.* Constantly put money away and understand your long-term plan. Try to stick to that plan and focus on growth over years rather than daily or weekly.

Warren Buffett considers patience a defining trait of success in investing. Impatient investors let anxiety and emotion rule their decision-making. A bias toward action can lead to detrimental investing behaviors. These detrimental behaviors include checking account balances too often, focusing on short-term market volatility, selling or buying at the wrong time, or abandoning a long-term strategic investment plan. These behaviors can damage investors' long-term returns.[50]

NINE OVERRIDING RULES ON INVESTING

THESE NINE RULES provide a set of basic investing principles to keep in mind:

1. Allocation is everything.
2. You must understand what you are investing in.
3. Develop a core plan for investment and define your core investments.
4. Assess whether to use an outside advisor and how to use the outside advisor or manager.
5. Understand your own temperament for investing and the distinction between behavioral finance and financial results.
6. Develop clarity about your investment goals.
7. Never borrow to invest in stocks.
8. Understand all your assets and how they impact your portfolio.
9. Bias toward a high degree of safety.

ALLOCATION AND UNDERSTANDING YOUR OWN MINDSET IS EVERYTHING

AS I WATCH the market drop periodically, I'm constantly reminded how important it is as a saver or an investor to do the work upfront to understand the risks inherent in different asset allocations and how you will respond when the market does different things. Now, in full disclosure, we are very much worriers when it comes to investments.

· · · · · · · · · · · · · · · · · · · ·
"If you have trouble imagining a 20% loss in the stock market, you shouldn't be in stocks."
– John Bogle, Founder, Vanguard[51]
· · · · · · · · · · · · · · · · · · · ·

The best way we have seen to understand and build an allocation is via Vanguard tools that can be found online. There you can

---

51 Selena Maranjian, "9 Investing Tips from Investing Icon John Bogle That You Shouldn't Ignore," The Motley Fool, March 19, 2020. https://www.fool.com/retirement/2020/03/19/9-investing-tips-from-investing-icon-john-bogle-th.aspx.

look at and adjust allocations of equities and debts to show both long-term returns as well as the number of years that the allocation will show a loss and a lot more.

If, like us, you can't mentally handle the down years very well, you may err in one direction versus the other, but you may also give up some upside. You can plug in almost any allocation you want into online investing tools, and then after you decide on the allocation you want, you will need to assess within those allocations where to put the funds. Within the categories, you also need to be very careful to pick the right assets.

The benefit of doing this work upfront is immense in terms of peace of mind during downturns and in not having to sell in times when the market is tanking.

There are plenty of great tools online that can show expected returns over longer periods of time based on allocations to stocks, bonds, and cash. The ultimate allocation for an actual person depends on a mix of analytical study of these tools and the emotional understanding of one's own makeup.

For example, the best long-term return may show a heavy allocation to equities or stocks. However, over shorter periods of time, this portfolio allocation may have many years where it loses money. Many investors handle those losses poorly. Thus, the actual optimal allocation for an individual or household usually reflects a mix of analytical finance and behavioral finance.

Many of the largest investment firms have fairly easy-to-use allocation tools. These can show under different periods of time how different allocations of equities versus bonds are likely to work out. For example, in a portfolio heavily weighted to stocks, over the long run you are likely to have higher returns than in an allocation weighted to bonds or cash. However, over certain periods of time, the ups and downs will be much higher than in a more balanced portfolio. In contrast, a portfolio highly weighted to bonds and cash will likely have fewer ups and downs but also will likely underperform a portfolio with heavier concentrations of equities over longer periods of time. But over short periods of time, it may lose a lot less value.

A key concept in investing is to have a consistent plan for how you invest. This can relate to how you allocate investments and what you invest in. Then, it's a regular discipline and challenge to try and stick to that discipline. The core investment plan drives the allocation of assets and the types of assets you invest in to match that allocation.

. . . .

"The best way to measure your investing success is not by whether you're beating the market but by whether you've put in place a financial plan and a behavioral discipline that are likely to get you where you want to go."
– Benjamin Graham, Financial Analyst,
Investor and Professor, known as
the "Father of Value Investing"[52]

. . . .

---

52 "Wisdom of Great Investors – Quotes," Davis ETFs. https://www.davisetfs.com/ investor_education/quotes.

········· **46** ·········

"CORE AND EXPLORE" INVESTMENT STRATEGY

HERE, THE CONCEPT is to have a few core parts of your investment strategy and portfolio that make up the vast majority of your holdings—i.e., 80% to 90%. Then, have a small percentage that you dabble or explore with.

In a world of endless choices, this is very helpful both financially and mentally. A good model is having a core composed of an S&P 500 index fund for growth over time and U.S. treasuries for safety and stability. For each person, the core may be different, but this is a good general concept.

Investment professionals suggest that the core-and-explore strategy has benefits for investors who largely believe in indexing but have an "active management itch" that they want to scratch. This is fairly common among younger investors who understand the rationale behind using low-cost investments for their core, but they still want the "thrill of outperformance" if they can get it by choosing actively managed funds for a small portion of their investment portfolio.[53]

53 Ilana Polyak, "Torn between active and passive? Try 'core and explore,'" CNBC, December 13, 2017. https://www.cnbc.com/2017/12/13/torn-between-active-and-passive-try-core-and-explore.html.

KNOW YOUR INVESTMENTS

MOST OF US should only invest in what we really know and understand. For example, it may make sense to invest in the S&P 500 as a broad market index and in treasuries and CDs as cash alternatives.

If, in contrast, you plan to invest in individual stocks or niche indexes or specific bonds like muni, corporate, or agency, you should really know the company or issuer and really try and understand the business and/or investment. Further, for most of us as individual investors, it is increasingly difficult to really know the issuers and companies.

Most of my worst investments have been made when I made an investment on a whim and without a clear thesis and understanding of why I was investing in something. In contrast, I have done far better when investing with great clarity around an area that I understand well.

• •

"Invest in what you know."
— Peter Lynch, Fidelity Investments[54]

• •

54 Matthew Frankel, CFP, "How to Invest Like Peter Lynch," The Motley Fool, November 20, 2023. https://www.fool.com/investing/how-to-invest/famous-investors/peter-lynch/.

······· **48** ·······

TIME IN THE MARKET VS. TIMING THE MARKET

MANY INVESTING PROFESSIONALS will say if you try to time the market, you'll probably end up losing in the long run by missing out on the key times and days when the market rises. When the market falls, it becomes very easy to think you need to remove money from the market. But history has shown that this is a bad idea, as pulling out on a dip—even a significant one—can lead to you losing out when the market swings back. Generally speaking, you want to periodically assess your allocation, allocate your assets in a way that matches your goals and risk tolerance, and then keep your assets in the market for the long run.

Before I understood how important my allocation and plan were, I would tend to be over-invested in equities. Then, when the market dropped, I might have a minor panic and sell some equities. This is a bad way to invest.

On the flip side, many wonder if they should "buy the dip." Buying when the market drops should ultimately be governed by your long-standing assessment of your portfolio allocation.

For example, if you have an intended allocation of 40/60 equities to bonds and cash and your allocation has fallen to 35/65, you probably should reallocate and might buy equities if there is a dip. If in contrast, if your intended allocation is 40/60 and your balances went up on equities and remains at 40/60 or above, you wouldn't buy the dip.

Here, at the end of the day there are two concepts at work. First, since one really never knows what a dip or the start of a long-term fall is, one should stick to their allocation principles. Second, in the long run, one wants their allocation correct, so stick to the overriding premise that time in the market is far more critical than timing the market.

· ·

"In the financial markets, hindsight is forever 20/20, but foresight is legally blind. And thus, for most investors, market timing is a practical and emotional impossibility."

– Benjamin Graham, investor and mentor to Warren Buffett[55]

· ·

55 Rachel Warrant, "15 Quotes That Prove Market Timing Is a Huge Mistake," The Motley Fool, August 14, 2022. https://www.fool.com/slideshow/15-quotes-that-prove-market-timing-is-a-huge-mistake/?slide=4.

THREE TYPES OF PORTFOLIOS

THESE EACH USE an S&P 500 index and U.S. Treasury Bonds as building blocks. This is oversimplified but is intended to help clarify directional guidance. The bonds in these cases would largely be one to five years in duration—relatively short term.

1. *Conservative - 5–20% S&P 500 and 80–95% in U.S. Treasury Bonds.* The hope is that the allocation to equities will help keep up with inflation and the allocation to bonds will provide income and safety. This portfolio would likely not gain as much over the longer term as other portfolios but would also not lose as much in shorter time frames.

2. *Balanced Portfolio - 40–60% in the S&P 500 index and the balance in U.S. Treasuries.* There is more room for growth than with the conservative portfolio, but also more room for losses.

3. *Growth Portfolio - 80–90% S&P 500 index and the balance in U.S. Treasury Bonds.* Here, you need the stomach to withstand short-term ups and downs, but the longer-term upside should be much more than the conservative or balanced portfolio.

Once you have established an investment plan and portfolio, try not to fall prey to "fear of missing out" or FOMO. All of us, myself included, have some regret that we missed the big, long term winning investment like Apple, Amazon, or NVIDIA. It would be inhuman not to feel some of this.

When the market surges or a stock surges or the reverse happens, however, the important thing is to understand your core investment plan. Try not to chase the winners or sell into a falling market. I did a lot of this early on. Over the years, I've matured my investment temperament and found it easier to keep the demons of FOMO at bay.

·········· 50 ··········
DO NOT BORROW TO INVEST IN STOCKS

ONE CORE RULE we live by is to never buy stocks on margin or with debt. Constantly look to limit debt and leverage. You will never be able to accurately predict when the market will climb or dip. Don't buy stocks with margin or debt.

In my view, debt and credit cards are awful things in general. Never borrow to invest in stocks and be conservative in all your borrowings. Debt kills countries, companies, and families.

········· **51** ·········

WHAT ABOUT BOND YIELDS?

MANY INVESTORS INCLUDE bonds in their portfolio because they are often less volatile than other asset classes like stocks. Using bonds for diversification can reduce portfolio volatility and risk.

A bond yield is the return an investor realizes on a bond. Bond yields are different from bond prices. The yield matches the coupon rate when the bond is issued. Price and yield are inversely related. As a result, when demand falls for bonds, yields or returns rise.

When fewer investors want bonds, issuers need to pay higher interest rates to encourage investors to buy bonds. When demand rises for bonds and the market for stocks is falling, the less issuers need to offer in interest payments and thus interest rates. So, the higher the demand for bonds, the lower the rates that issuers have to offer and the lower the yields and returns from bonds.

THE TWO TYPES OF RISK IN BONDS—DURATION OR INTEREST RATE RISK AND CREDIT RISK

WHEN INVESTING IN bonds, it's important to understand two types of risk:

1. *Interest rate risk.* This refers to owning a bond with a certain yield and having market yields rise above that yield. Then, the current bonds one owns go down in their value. The longer the duration, the higher the risk.

2. *Credit risk.* This refers to the risk that the issuer will suffer financially and not be able to make its interest or principal payments.

Understanding interest rate risk and duration risk is really important. People invest in treasury and safer bonds to not lose money. But you can lose a lot of money if you invest in bonds or bond funds and interest rates rise. It's important to understand how the value of a bond changes if rates go up or down.

10 NOTES ON PRIVATE EQUITY VS. VENTURE CAPITAL

MANY PEOPLE HEAR about venture capital (VC) and private equity (PE) in the mainstream press. While most individual investors—especially those just getting started—aren't likely to participate in a VC or PE investment, it is still beneficial to understand how they work. For individuals with higher net worth, VC and PE can represent attractive investments.

When I first started to be invited to invest in private equity and venture capital funds, I thought, "Wow, I have really reached the big time and I'm a real investor." Then I learned several lessons:

- All PE funds are not the same. Some are great and some are awful.

- Getting into funds such as Andreessen Horowitz as an investor was harder than getting admitted to Harvard Law School.

- Large, great funds will take individual money, but they really live on institutional investors.

- Your money is tied up for a long time and you have no control over it.

- The funds that do great over one set of years are often not the funds that do great in the next set of years.

Questions are often asked about similarities and differences between private equity and venture capital investing. Here are 10 observations:

1. Both private equity and venture capital funds are largely investing in companies that are not publicly traded. At one time, it was thought of as exclusively so, but increasingly or periodically, there are PIPEs—private investments in public entities—or leveraged buyouts that will sometimes take a public company private.

2. Venture capital is typically investing in earlier-stage companies. These companies can be pre-revenue and are generally pre-profit. Many of the more sophisticated venture capital firms are investing in companies that they hope can reach massive scale.

3. Unlike venture capital, private equity is generally investing in established companies that have profits. The companies receiving private equity investments can be of any size and scope as well.

4. Venture capital generally invests with straight equity. Debt is kept out of the picture.

5. Most private equity investors rely on a mix of equity and debt. Leverage is very important to amplify the total return.

6. An investment by a venture capital fund is more likely to be binary in nature with success (or not). That is, a small percentage of the investments generate a very disproportionate amount of the returns to the fund.

7. A private equity firm expects most of its investments to perform well and expects very few to fail. Here, the firm and any fund will also have a divergence of returns. Most funds will make 7 to 15 investments in companies. Some of those will do great, some will do fine, and a few may do poorly.

8. Large pension funds, endowments, and insurance firms have a proportion of their investments in private equity and venture capital with a higher amount in private equity than venture capital.

9. Venture capital investments are generally seen as higher risk than private equity investments. This is because venture capital investments are typically in earlier-stage companies while private equity is in established companies that are already producing profits.

10. Family offices and high-net-worth families will also have a portion of their portfolio in private equity and venture capital.

······ *Section 8* ······

FREEDOM FOR LIFE?

············

BECOMING FINANCIALLY WISE

······························

BECOMING FINANCIALLY WISE
(CHAPTERS 54-60)

In the last section, we focused on building wealth. This section focuses on the importance of overall financial literacy and financial health—so you have the money and financial stability to be able to live the fulfilling life you want, now and into retirement.

Important concepts include living within your means, putting money away, having emergency funds, preparing for recessions, and thinking through your financial situation well in advance of retirement so you can enjoy your retirement.

It's important to think about these issues. Rich people go broke too. We have had the chance to watch people who made tens of millions of dollars go broke. I watched a close colleague blow a fortune through buying boats, big houses, and more. Thankfully, he made the fortune again and was able to hold on to that fortune. Watching these things happen, however, was very scary and instructive for me. It led me to be much more careful.

LIVE WITHIN YOUR MEANS; PAY YOURSELF FIRST

HERE, ONE NEEDS to be aggressive about living within one's means and saving money each month. Living within your means applies at every level of wealth. I've known people who have sold businesses for $80 million and found themselves in financial trouble. I couldn't understand it until they told me about their $15 million house, their huge boat, and more.

If you want to be independent, the key concept is to spend less than you make. This thought comes from *Richer, Wiser, Happier* by William Green. "Financial independence doesn't come from making or having lots of money ... It comes from spending less than you make."[56]

Learning this discipline is very important when people are young. It's very easy to outspend your money. And as one gets older, many people become very concerned about outliving their

---

56 William Green. https://williamgreenwrites.com/.

money. If you want to be affluent or wealthy, work to make more, keep your spending in check, and invest a good percentage of your income constantly.

HAVE A JOB OR BUSINESS AND PUT MONEY AWAY OUTSIDE THE JOB OR BUSINESS

A core goal is to develop net worth outside of your business or job. For example, many lawyers or professionals also invest in real estate, the stock market, or other businesses. The long-term goal is to become financially independent of your core job or business.

An overriding concept is to keep investing and putting money away so you have a net worth outside of your job or business along with your job or business.

According to Warren Buffett, consistent investing from a young age has a snowball effect. He says it's like "being at the top of a very large hill with wet snow and starting a snowball and getting it rolling downhill."[57]

57 Sarah Berger, "Manage your money like the super-wealthy – 3 habits to steal from Warren Buffett, Mark Cuban and Kevin O'Leary," CNBC, August 20, 2018. https://www.cnbc.com/2018/08/20/how-to-manage-your-money-like-the-super-wealthy.html.

······· **56** ·········

IF YOU WANT TO BE RICH

SCHWAB ANNUALLY CONDUCTS a survey of Americans about what it takes to be "wealthy" and financially comfortable. In 2022, respondents said it takes an average net worth of $2.2 million to be considered wealthy.

There's a big difference between being really well off financially to being under water. Happiness for the most part—and studies show this—doesn't greatly change from one to the other. That stated, the ability to take care of family and friends and emergencies increases with financial health.

In my observation—and I'm excluding people born into a lot of money—most fortunes are made through owning one's own business. We've also seen people get very wealthy in the private equity or venture capital sector or in the technology business. Many real estate developers have also done really well.

The world constantly changes as to where the opportunities are. One constant is that it's easier to become really well off through ownership of a business. In looking at business ownership, many people keep their job and test different business opportunities. I don't personally promote the "all or nothing" approach or "burn the boats" approach. I'm also a believer in minimizing debt.

EMERGENCY FUNDS ARE CRITICAL

HAVING EMERGENCY SAVINGS is extremely important. Unexpected events can occur, like losing a job, falling ill or having a loved one become ill, or living through a natural disaster. These events can have a devastating financial impact. Unfortunately, many people don't have enough emergency funds to deal with these types of situations.

Here are some thoughts about emergency funds:

- Whatever you think you need for an emergency fund, you should double it at least.

- Your emergency fund should be in readily accessible money market funds.

- You should look at your stocks-to-bonds allocation after you account for your emergency fund. Let's say that you have $100,000 in an emergency fund and $500,000 of money that you can invest. You should think outside of the $100,000. Think of the $500,000 as what you are allocating.

- Your investment advisor makes more the more you invest. Don't let them goad you out of having a substantial emergency fund.

No one ever thinks an emergency will affect them, but emergencies occur without warning every day.

A significant portion of Americans don't have an emergency fund with even three months of expenses. A May 2023 survey conducted by Bankrate and SSRS found that 57% of adults in the United States are uncomfortable with their current emergency savings and 33% are very uncomfortable.[58]

Every individual and household should maintain an emergency fund of a minimum of six months of living expenses or more. Obviously, the more, the better, within reason. This should be in easily accessible liquid assets and ideally non-risky defensive assets.

---

58 Lane Gillespie, "Bankrate's 2023 annual emergency savings report," Bankrate, June 22, 2023. https://www.bankrate.com/banking/savings/emergency-savings-report/.

SIX WAYS TO PREPARE FOR A RECESSION

WHEN THE ECONOMY is going well, it seems like good times will go on forever. However, since the end of World War II, the United States has experienced 12 recessions. That's a recession on average every 6.5 years.[59] Because recessions are inevitable and occur about once per decade, it's important to think proactively about preparing for these downturns.

Here are six suggestions:

1. *Keep your job secure.* Make sure you are doing great at your job and perform the best you can.

2. *Look for ways to cut your spending.* Try to be less vulnerable to job loss or lower income.

---

59 Dan Burrows, "What is a Recession? 10 Facts You Need to Know," Kiplinger, November 2, 2023. https://www.kiplinger.com/slideshow/investing/t038-s001-recessions-10-facts-you-must-know/index.html.

3. *Work to develop an emergency savings fund.* This is money that would be in cash or other liquid amounts and not in equities.

4. *Evaluate the composition of your portfolio.* Make sure you have an allocation of equities and treasury bonds that you can live with in good and bad times.

5. *Look to pay down debt.* Here, balance this with the goal of having a large emergency fund of cash. Don't deplete your emergency fund to pay down debt.

6. *Don't make big rash moves under stress.* Cut monthly expenses, pay down debt, and develop emergency savings.

SIX KEY CONCEPTS FOR RETIREMENT

MOST PEOPLE DREAM about some type of retirement. However, anyone who has gotten to my age knows plenty of people and families that have found themselves unable to retire or in financial trouble. Further, as one gets older it's harder and harder to make money or have money compound for you.

Aside from what's written here, it's critical to find ways to put away money early and often. So many people I know said they would save later and they never got around to it. It's also very important to manage your financial investment risk. To be successful in the long run, you need to find the right balance for you that helps your assets grow and also protects enough of them just in case. Everyone needs to learn to live on less than they make.

Here are six ideas to keep in mind as you think about the transition from work to retirement:

1. Make sure current expenses are in line with expected income.

2. Aim for sufficient assets that can generate interest and be enough to draw down over the expected course of your retirement—from the time you stop working until the time you pass away. Err on the side of overestimating your needs.

3. Plan for known expenses and anticipate some level of unexpected expenses.

4. Reduce debt fully or at least make sure your debt doesn't have a lot of variable rate exposure to it.

5. Plan for some level of inflation in your assessments.

6. Assure your investment strategy doesn't leave you overexposed to too much risk.

········· **60** ·········

THE 4% RULE

"Cut your retirement spending now," *Wall Street Journal* writer Anne Tergesen says.[60] Tergesen writes about the creator of the 4% rule, William Bengen, and his perspective.

The 4% rule says for a 30-year retirement, you can take out 4% a year. Bengen has said that at certain times, given stock valuation increases, challenges, and lower inflation, you could even take out more and still be safe for 30 years. More recently, Bengen has said that the 4% rule could leave people in poor financial shape and has recommended taking out less principal each year.

To put it as simply as possible, a core goal is to delay taking out money or spending down your retirement nest egg for as long as possible. Things can snowball in the wrong direction much quicker than you expect. Not spending down the principal requires tremendous discipline. The more you put away for retirement and the longer you delay spending it down, the better.

---

60 Anne Tergesen, "Cut Your Retirement Spending Now, Says Creator of the 4% Rule," *The Wall Street Journal*, April 19, 2022. https://www.wsj.com/articles/cut-your-retirement-spending-now-says-creator-of-the-4-rule-11650327097.

The 4% rule was originally created for investors with a 30-year retirement horizon. The simplifying assumptions it uses for future returns, diversification, and fees can limit the viability of a retirement plan over shorter and longer time horizons.[61]

61 Paulo Costa, Ph.D., et al., "Fuel for the F.I.R.E.: Updating the 4% rule for early retirees," Vanguard Research, June 2021. https://corporate.vanguard.com/content/dam/corp/research/pdf/Fuel-for-the-F.I.R.E.-Updating-the-4-rule-for-early-retirees-US-ISGFIRE_062021_Online.pdf.

ACKNOWLEDGMENTS

A **SPECIAL THANK** you goes out to family, including Liz, Chloe, Bobby, Ross, Jordy, Billy, Hannah, Mort, Naomi, Mady, Fred, Lyn, Bob, Jami, Glenn, Elise, and Cindy.

A second big thank you is given to colleagues at Becker's Healthcare, particularly Jessica Cole, Katie Atwood, Annie Stokes, Ally Warner, Molly Gamble, Laura Dyrda, Emma Bulwa, Margo Vieceli, Scott Jones, Abbie Engel, Kelly Gooch, Mackenzie Bean, Brian Zimmerman, Ginny Egizio, Ryan Ciepley, Haley Jones, Cierra Levy, Taylor Possley, Jack Burns, Maura Taylor, Daniel Gest, Sarah Simon, Peter Kryzwosz, Malena McClory, Molly Traverso, Kristelle Khazzaka, and many, many more.

Another big thank you goes to leaders and colleagues at McGuireWoods, including Amber Walsh, Holly Buckley, Bart Walker, Geoff Cockrell, Melissa Szabad, Gretchen Townshend, Anna Timmerman, Helen Suh, Tim Fry, David Pivnick, Jeff Clark, and leaders outside of healthcare, such as Tracy Walker,

Rick Viola, Jon Harmon, Tom Cabaniss, David Pusateri, Richard Cullen, Bill Burress, and William Strickland.

Finally, there is a group of people from different parts of my business life who I have really benefited from and who have been very inspiring and insightful to me. Thank you. These include Barry Tanner, Dr. Brent Lambert, Luke Lambert, Tom Mallon, Andrew Hayek, Joe Zasa, Lisa Rock, Nader Samii, JP Gallagher, Lloyd Dean, Venkat Mocherla, Manav Sevak, Jeff Hillebrand, Gary Weiss, Paul Summerside, Nancy Agee, Gene Woods, Nancy Temple, Kelly Jo McArthur, Bob Burnstine, Rob Benun, Marc Benjamin, Brian Levy, Mark Abramson, David Abramson, Dr. Jeff Bergman, Julie Yoo, David Mack, Dr. Stephen Klasko, Dr. David Feinberg, Michael Dowling, Chris Van Gordor, Joe Gutman, Andy Friedman, David Stafman, Teri Fontenot, Lou Shapiro, Michael Sachs, Chuck Lauer, Howard Kern, Michael Ugwueke, Rick Levin, Stan Slovin, Howard Sutker, Eric Schloss, Mark Sibul, Eric Cooper, Marc Blum, Jim Field, Mark Krasnow, Karen McHenry, Vineeta Agarwala, Scott Stevens, Art Roselle, Justin Ishbia, Jeremy Corr, Chanell Bunger, Kirsten Doell, and many more. Thank you. Thank you. Thank you.

ABOUT THE AUTHORS

SCOTT BECKER

Scott Becker is the founder, publisher, and chief content officer of Becker's Healthcare, a leading healthcare media company. Scott is also a long-time partner at McGuireWoods, a top AmLaw firm with leading private equity and healthcare practices. He served for nearly 14 years as the chair of the healthcare department and also served on the Board of Directors. Mr. Becker has interviewed Bill and Hilary Clinton, George and Laura Bush, Nikki Haley, Kareem Abdul Jabbar, Venus Williams, and many other public figures.

Scott is a graduate of Harvard Law School and the University of Illinois. At Harvard Law School he had the privilege to teach and advise future President Barack Obama as a moot court adviser. The President was much more gifted than Mr. Becker. He hosts the highly-ranked *Becker's Healthcare Podcast* and the highly-ranked *Becker Private Equity* Podcast. He is also the author of several books, a regular speaker on business and healthcare trends, a proponent of physical and mental health as a foundation for life, and an active investor in private equity and venture capital funds and companies. Mr. Becker is a regular but not particularly accomplished golfer and tennis player. He has also coached tennis for several years.

GRACE LYNN KELLER

Grace Lynn Keller is a graduate of the University of Iowa with degrees in journalism and mass communication and a certificate in writing. As Vice President of marketing and production company Executive Podcast Solutions, Grace enjoys using her unique skillset to help clients from around the world find their voice, tell their stories, and develop their brand. Grace also served as Miss Iowa 2021 and represented the state at the centennial Miss America Pageant. During her year of service, she traveled over 30,000 miles to bring literacy programming to Iowa's rural and low-income school districts and community libraries under her service platform, Read to Succeed. In her free time, Grace enjoys reading fiction novels, experimenting in the kitchen with new recipes, and sharing her love of ballet, an art in which she spent 16 years training in while growing up.

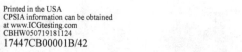

9 798990 566101